EUROPE BLOODY EUROPE

D1080894

Previous published works:

Noost
Scotland Bloody Scotland
The Tupper Report

EUROPE BLOODY EUROPE

An illustrated, brief and waspish
History of Britain's
E.C. partners.

THE BARON OF RAVENSTONE

CANONGATE

First published in 1992 by
Canongate Press Plc,
14 Frederick Street, Edinburgh

Text and Illustrations © Frank Renwick of Ravenstone

British Library Cataloguing-in-Publication Data.
A catalogue record for this book is available from
the British Library.

ISBN 0 86241 370 2

Typeset by Falcon Typographic Art Ltd, Fife, Scotland
Printed and bound by Billings, Worcester

PREFACE

On the surface, Britain's E.C. chums are a pretty mixed bag historically speaking. There's the French with their insufferable sense of cultural superiority, their paranoid, unattractive kings and l'Empereur Napoleon. There's the Dutch, who are more amphibians than humans, the Spanish Inquisition, the Italians with their war record, the Irish for God's sake and, of course, the Germans. A pretty dire lot, and that's not saying much about the Belgians with their everlasting linguistic quarrels, the pig-rearing Danes, the Greeks, the Luxemburgers and the Portuguese, about all of whom no one seems to know anything much. Little wonder that Mrs Thatcher, Mr Ridley and many other persons of worth and standing have expressed dismay at the prospect of being federated together with these types, under the diktat of an even grosser bureaucracy than we have already.

This book does not gloss over unpleasant facts with sugary pink whitewash. By giving the histories of our E.C. partners a vigorous airing it provides the essential historical background to a more realistic understanding of today's European Community. History has dealt most of our partners a much bloodier hand than Britain has ever held: it has also been a richer cultural hand in many ways. Each is unique, but what each shares with the others is worth finding out. For the author, the long, valiant and commendably ingenious resistance of the Belgians and Italians to bureaucracy is one of the hopeful attractions of federation.

The real problem is not Europeans but our abysmal lack of understanding about Europe (and its languages). We simply cannot categorise Spain as the land of Inquisition: Italians do not spend all their lives running away. And Germany – which has always needed watching – is treasure better shared than encircled. Certainly there is no cause to regard federation as a young bridegroom eyeth his bride, but there is every possible reason to join in wholeheartedly. We should not be joining total strangers for an uncertain future: we should be among friends with more to give us than we have to give them. And chances like that do not come often. History proves it.

Frank Renwick of Ravenstone

Gegen Bürokraten
Helfen nur Soldaten.

Belgium

The Belgians are uniquely used to other Europeans. They have had them traipsing in and out of their country since time immemorial, taxing it, looting it and butchering its inhabitants at frequent intervals since Roman times.

The *Belgae*, according to Great Caesar, were Celts like everyone else in those days. He conquered them in 52 BC, and praises them as the bravest of the Gauls, which probably meant they were exceptionally stubborn. That is what they have remained ever since in the teeth of continual foreign domination, and if they hadn't been masters of the art they'd have disappeared long ago. The Romans were there for four hundred years, and even in those days the Belgae exhibited a flair for commercial expertise: Belgic textiles were exported in quantity all over the Empire.

When the Roman Empire collapsed in the fifth century, the Belgae were invaded by the Franks who conquered all Gaul and established their Merovingian kingdom. By the eighth century, an astute Belgian, Pepin of Heristal started taking over from the Merovingians. His son, Charles Martel smashed the Islamic conquest of Western Europe at the Battle of Poitiers in 732, and his grandson, Charlemagne, re-established a Western Empire in 800. This in turn disintegrated and in 843, by the Treaty of Verdun, his grandsons split it into three kingdoms: France, Germany and Lotharingia – named after Lothar, the eldest brother – an unlikely swathe stretching from the Netherlands to northern Italy, its name perpetuated in the border province of Lorraine (Lothringen in German).

In Belgium, the boundary ran along the river Scheldt, so that Flanders was separated from the rest of the territory in the French side of the border, and the division thus created by a Dark Age treaty is with Belgium to this day. The population is not racially divided, but part speaks a Germanic language, Flemish, and part speaks French.

With central government weak or non-existent, and invasions and mayhem rife, local barons carved out strongholds and fiefs for themselves. Such a one was Baldwin Iron Arm, first Count of Flanders, 862, who fought off Viking attacks on his coasts and up the great rivers of the Low Countries.

A yet more famous Belgian feudal noble was Gottfried von Bouillon (in the Ardennes). In response to Pope Urban's call to save the Holy Land from the infidel, he sold estates on the Meuse, pledged his castle at Bouillon to the Bishop of Liège, blackmailed the Jews, and equipped by these efforts a sizeable army for the First Crusade. And off, at the end of August 1096, he went, with permission from his overlord, the German Emperor Henry IV. With him went his brothers Eustace III, Count of Boulogne, and Baldwin, the landless younger brother, who took his wife and children with him because he did not intend to return. They were joined by many other leading knights from Belgian territory: Baldwin of Rethel, Baldwin Count of Hainault, Rainald Count of Toul, Dudo of Konz-Saarburg and many another gallant besides. Two Flemish knights, Litold and Gilbert of Tournai, were the first Crusaders to enter the Holy City at the final siege, and they were closely followed by Gottfried himself, who was then chosen to rule Jerusalem. Yet there are people who say there have been no famous Belgians.

Back home, despite the efforts of various German – Holy Roman – Emperors and assorted Kings of France to control the area, autonomous baronial fiefdoms flowered unchecked. Even the power of the Counts of Flanders was waning by mid-thirteenth century. It was time for the emergence of the bourgeoisie, and the Belgians took to it like ducks to water. Their land contained the estuaries of great waterways – the Rhine, the Meuse, the Scheldt – all of them useful shipping routes into northern Europe for those, such as the English, who might wish to avoid far longer journeys in little leaky boats into the Baltic or the Mediterranean. By 1256, Bruges with its excellent position on the now

vanished Zwin had secured a valuable monopoly of the English wool and cloth trade and had become a central entrepôt for German and Lombard bankers who came there to establish profitable businesses. Liège became renowned for arms manufacture. Ghent and Ypres grew wealthy on fine cloth manufactured from English wool imported through Bruges. The absence of strong external government was a key factor in the growth of these towns, for their citizens were in a position to give their full loyalty to their cities alone, which, as in Ancient Greece, were each its own mini-state. Rich merchants gave fortunes to enhance their own towns with splendid Gothic guild halls, colleges, belfries and churches.

From the feudal point of view, this was all very reprehensible, and from the point of view of Philip the Fair, King of France, it was positively alarming that his neighbours were making so much money. In 1302, he made a truce with his enemy, Edward I, King of England, and invaded Flanders to crush these upstart cities and confiscate their wealth. At the Battle of the Golden Spurs fought near Kortrijk (Courtrai) in southern Flanders, the gilded cavalry of France received a complete and thoroughly laudable kicking from the stout burghers. It was the Flemings' finest hour, and is celebrated annually to this day.

Their triumph, however, was short-lived. Without a strong overlord, they were too rich to be left in peace. At the start of the Hundred Years War period (1340–1453), Edward III of England, married to Philippa of Hainault, 'borrowed' immense sums in ready cash from international bankers in Belgium and used a lot of it to take a score of local nobles onto his payroll. As France used Scotland, so the English now hoped to use Belgium as a convenient client state and back door base. But his plan to gain complete control of Belgium by a marriage between his son and Margaret, the heiress to Flanders, was scotched by Urban V, a French puppet Pope. Instead, Margaret married the French King's brother, Philip the Bold, Duke of Burgundy, and so began the ascendancy in Belgium of a house that was to rival France itself and become a glittering new Lotharingia.

Politically, the Duke's power was supreme: occasional revolts were smacked down, as at Dinant (which was sacked) and Liège (which was razed to the ground). The ducal court at Bruges was the exemplar for the whole of Europe of courtly dress, magnificence and etiquette. For Burgundy, by absorbing Belgium, was the richest state in Europe. Kings and great barons vied to emulate the cut of the latest Burgundian doublet, to possess sumptuous Flemish manuscripts, to have their portraits painted by Memling or Van der Goes.

But it was all to vanish like snow off a dyke. There came a time when France was no longer ruled by weaklings and idiots, when cunning, sinister Louis XI proved more than a match diplomatically for Duke Charles the Rash in his attempts to unite his eleven provinces in the Low Countries with Burgundy and Franche-Comté via Alsace and Lorraine. Abandoned by his allies, Charles was slain at the Battle of Nancy in 1477, leaving his daughter Mary of Burgundy to face a revolt of the Belgian communes and the continuing intrigues of Louis XI. To the rebels Mary issued the Great Privilege of Ghent confirming to the cities the rights and privileges they had lost under Burgundy. To Louis she administered the slap in the face of marrying Maximilian of Austria, the first of 350 years of Habsburgs to rule in the Low Countries. Then, unfortunately, she died, in 1482, still only twenty-four years old, in a riding accident.

Maximilian was unable to establish his authority without her in Brabant and Flanders, and the independent Estates of the communes concluded the Peace of Arras with Louis in 1482, whereby Mary's infant daughter was betrothed to the Dauphin, and huge chunks of Burgundian territory went to France. The most glittering prize, possession of Belgium, had eluded the French yet again – greatly to the chagrin of the spider-like Louis – but he had certainly ended Burgundian independence and splendour.

From now on Belgium was to be tied in, overruled, harried and milked under various branches of the imperial Habsburg family, experts of long standing in the art of acquiring other people's land by marriage. Maximilian, who used his German mercenaries to impose his will on Ghent, Bruges and Aix, became Emperor in 1492, when his son Philip took over control of the Low Countries and, in 1496, married Juanna the Mad, daughter and heiress of Ferdinand and Isabella of Spain. From this union emerged a Habsburg empire that stretched eventually from the Turkish frontier to the Philippines, an unbelievable concept in 1496 but an actual fact when, in 1519, Philip and Juanna's son Charles was crowned Holy Roman Emperor (Charles V) and inherited the lot.

Although Belgium was but a tiny corner of this, the biggest empire in history, the Emperor Charles, who had been born in Ghent, remained deeply

attached to the land of his birth and appointed able regents. The Belgians, ever pragmatic and capable of profitable compromise, did not sit around moping for their lost freedoms: they saw the unrivalled commercial opportunities of the vast new empire with its untold wealth and undiscovered territories. Their rivals the Italian cities, particularly Venice, were now going into decline, the Mediterranean being no longer the centre of world trade. Thus it was the counting houses of Antwerp that financed the spice trade and the colonisation of the Americas, forged new trade routes to the East and shipped Flemish cloth throughout the known world. Flemish sea-farers and geographers, such as Mercator (Gerhard Kremer), helped redraw the world. Wealth increased. Artists of the calibre of Pieter Breughel and Hieronymus Bosch mirrored the age and its preoccupations in fantastic detail. And with wealth came a heightened level of discontent.

There were frictions during the time of the Emperor Charles: over increased taxation to pay for military confrontations with France, over the increasingly arbitrary style of the imperial bureaucracy – the Belgians have had to deal with more bureaucracies than any other race on earth – and over suspicions that rigorous Counter-Reformation Catholicism was replacing traditional tolerance. But Charles was a pragmatist and, besides, he had been born in Ghent. It was when he retired worn out to a Spanish monastery in 1555 that the real trouble started. His son and successor, King Philip II of Spain, was a Catholic zealot of the worst sort, entirely Spanish in outlook, believing that the cause of Spain

MIND YOU: I'VE HEARD MERCATOR'S PROJECTION ISN'T WHAT IT WAS.

was the Cause of God. He was certainly no Belgian: not only could he not speak Flemish, he couldn't even speak French. His policy from the start was to stamp out all political or religious dissent: his introduction of the notorious Inquisition and his execution of dissident nobles were the sparks that ignited the Low Countries. It was an age of horrific religious fanaticism.

By the mid 1560s, the whole of the Low Countries was in revolt, and a protracted war developed. Despite his apparently limitless resources and military superiority, under the command of the cruel Duke of Alba, Philip paradoxically lacked cash and effective sea power, but by the late '70s his Italian general, Alessandro Farnese, split the resistance. In 1579, Hainault, Artois, Douai surrendered, and others in the pro-Catholic south followed. With the surrender of Antwerp in 1585, Belgium was back in the Habsburg fold, and the seven undefeated Protestant United Provinces in the north were left to form an independent republic.

Culturally, the golden age lingered on into the early seventeenth century, the age of Van Dyke and Rubens with his great lardy women, and Teniers with his blowsy clowns, but the spirit had been stamped out of the Belgians. The Dutch were the people of the future, and by 1640 their navy had closed the Scheldt totally to international shipping, so that Antwerp and all the rest withered and grew grassy and hopeless in the lengthening Spanish shade. Spanish wealth proved a terrible illusion, an immensity of gold and silver raped from the New World and thrown away on wars, huge buildings and idle clerics. France seized large areas along the southern frontier while the Spanish empire declined rapidly into crazy, tottering decay.

From 1650 till 1830 therefore, Belgium became and remained a provincial

TELL YOU WHAT, PIET.
HOW ABOUT A POPPY FACTORY?

backwater. The great powers continued to fight each other back and forth over her territory. When Louis XIV engineered the Bourbon takeover of Spain in 1700, the War of Spanish Succession ended with the Peace of Utrecht in 1713, which severed Belgium from Spain and handed it over to the Austrian Habsburgs. Despite their well-meaning efforts, the country remained stagnant. Indeed when a Franco-Irish army effectively won it during the next war (1745), the economic decline was seen to be so dire that the French handed it back to the Austrians again at the Peace of Aix-la-Chapelle in 1748.

It took the French Revolution to set the cat among the bourgeois pigeons. In 1790, the Belgians with revolutionary fervour upped and proclaimed a United States of Belgium, whereupon the Austrians promptly suppressed it. It is a platitude that revolutionary governments find their major successes in carrying out the policies of their overthrown predecessors. The French had been trying to take over Belgium since the Dark Ages. The ancien régime was no sooner drowned in its own blood than the revolutionary government overran Belgium, Luxemburg and the Netherlands in the name of Liberty. Unlike her northern neighbour, Belgium was not allowed a separate identity in this new age of Reason but was reorganised as a department of the French state, and so remained till 1815 when her pre-eminent facilities as a battleground were used once again for the battle of Waterloo, near Brussels.

The resulting Congress of Vienna in 1815, designed to set Europe to rights after all the revolutionary and Napoleonic turmoil, 'reunited' Belgium to the

THERE'S ONE THING ABOUT THE FRENCH STEPHANIE. EVERY TIME THEY COME THEY HAVE A DIFFERENT STORY.

Netherlands – to which she had never been united in the first place – a decision which the Dutch greeted warmly, but which hardly went down a treat with the conservative, Catholic nationalists in Belgium. There were riots in Brussels, a provisional government was formed, a national congress elected, the black, red and gold flag of Brabant was raised for the nation and in 1830 the Dutch were driven out. As ever, the French moved in and by intrigue got the Duke of Nemours, brother of the French King Louis Philippe, elected King. Then Lord Palmerston – Britain being very much Top Dog in 1830 – gave everyone a smart rap across the knuckles. At the Congress of London in 1830, Belgium became an independent kingdom in the British mode, with Palmerston's choice – Leopold of Saxe-Coburg-Gotha – as King. Belgium's neutrality was guaranteed by all the Great Powers, including Prussia: not that that prevented the Dutch invading in 1839 over boundary disputes. They were driven out by the virtuous French.

Culturally, the new country was stuffily French, bourgeois and myopic, but it was also in some ways a British protégé. It aimed to be an industrial power and very soon become one, its industry based on the coal, iron, steel, glass, textile and ship-building of the southern, French-speaking provinces. Under Leopold II it acquired the Congo (an acquisition entirely financed by Leopold because his subjects were too short-sighted to see the potential) and became, like Britain and France, a colonial power with vast mineral and forest resources in the Dark Continent. Belgium's two main weaknesses were: the deepening division between the French-speaking Brussels élite and the Flemish-speaking population of the northern provinces, tied as they were to a declining rural economy and becoming very definitely second-class citizens in their own country; and defence.

The later nineteenth century was the first prolonged period of peace the Belgians had experienced since the great days of the Duchy of Burgundy, and the politicians felt assured it would last forever. Yet Prussia was already on her borders, with a Belgian enclave incorporated in her territory by the Congress of Vienna, and the creation of Bismarck's Reich as well as the unpredictable adventurism of Napoleon III were clearly seen as threats by Leopold II. His politicians didn't agree: defence budgets were cut again and again; frontier forts remained on paper; and there were protracted arguments about conscription when Leopold proposed it.

In 1909, Albert, son of the Count of Flanders, succeeded his uncle, Leopold II. 1914 proved who was right, but by then it was too late. The big armies were back trampling over the country and destroying everything in their paths, only this time mechanised warfare meant it was not just a re-run of the War of the Spanish Succession. The war was a war of stalemate, of attrition, of pounding the ancient cities into the mud. The killings were in millions: a quarter of a million British troops alone died in Flanders. Some of the Flemish population welcomed the Germans as deliverers from Walloon domination. King Albert fought on after his country's defeat, with the British and the French. When the Allies eventually won with American backing, the country had been devastated, there was bitter anti-Flemish feeling, and the government ended Belgian neutrality by a treaty with France in 1919.

The inter-war years were beset with economic and industrial problems. The southern coalfields never recovered, iron ore ran out, heavy industries sickened, labour unrest mushroomed. The dominance of the French-speaking Walloons therefore slackened, while in Flanders new scientific farming methods boosted output and new light industries sprang up around ancient Antwerp.

During the next German occupation (1940–5) there was again considerable pro-German support, at least to begin with, whilst others joined the resistance or fought abroad. King Leopold III, the first Flemish-speaking monarch, did not choose the heroic path of King Albert but chose a much harder role: he stayed to mitigate the severity of Nazi occupation. He did all he could throughout these years to secure better conditions, even going to Berchtesgaden and pleading with Hitler. It is estimated that he saved over 500,000 from deportation to German slave factories by such actions. In 1944 he was arrested by the SS and removed to Germany.

The King's conduct reinforced the split in Belgium between Flemings and Walloons: the former thoroughly supported his role throughout the war, the latter passionately denounced it as pro-Nazi, and when the politicians returned from their safe exile in 1945 they were determined to make Leopold a scapegoat for their own abysmal policies in the inter-war years. The country became more and more divided. In a referendum on the King's future in 1950, 57 per cent voted in favour of Leopold, but the Walloon provinces and the Brussels area had a majority against. There were demonstrations, strikes and Socialist rallies. Rather than drive his countrymen into further antagonisms, Leopold abdicated in favour of his son, the present King Baudouin (Baldwin). It was not pleasant, but it was an essentially Belgian compromise.

The present reign has seen a determinedly bi-cultural state develop, where neither group predominates and power is shared between the regions. Belgians have had to compromise and co-operate throughout their history, or they would long ago have been absorbed by their bullying neighbours. It is hardly an accident therefore that she has developed a role as the centre for European co-operation. There was already a Belgium-Luxemburg economic union in 1921. In 1948 came the Benelux Union between these two and the Netherlands. NATO was hatched in Brussels (1948–9) and when de Gaulle withdrew from it in 1966 the headquarters was transferred from Paris to Brussels. In 1951, a heavy industries common market, the European Coal, Iron & Steel Community, was established with a common programme of expansion. In 1955 the delegates of Belgium, West Germany, France, the Netherlands, Italy and Luxemburg met at Messina and agreed to form the European Economic Community. From the start, as the Treaty of Rome (1957) states, a closer union of European peoples was the aim, an end to the endless rivalries of past centuries, a real community of interest, not merely a Common Market.

Today Brussels is both the traditional heart of Brabant and a boomtown for Eurocrats. The people are both modern and thoroughly, unashamedly conservative, in their religion, their family life, their celebrations of ancient victories and past trials. Compromise has been their lifeblood for a very long time: so has form-filling, bureaucracy and an inbred genius for dealing with it. They are a resilient people the Belgians, and the Eurocrats are as likely to take them over permanently as any of the other swarms of locusts the Belgians have borne in the past. To a Belgian, the one-step-forward-two-steps-back dance of the timid British has been a source of considerable merriment.

 denmark

Only the Danes and the Irish among European Community members were never conquered by, or brought into prolonged commercial contact with the Romans. As a result both nations have retained a feyness, a trollishness from more ancient, beech-wooded times which has certainly helped them on occasion to triumph over grim realities.

Not that the Danes were always the jolly pig- and dairy-farmers they are today. Virtually unheard-of before the eighth century, they then launched themselves successfully upon Dark Age Europe as Vikings, and particularly political Vikings at that, not only looting and raping abroad in the first outburst of European tourism but conquering some very sizeable territories far from their native heath. They conquered almost the whole of England till Alfred the Great regained the southern half of it in 886, whereafter the north remained Danelaw till 1066. They conquered Normandy from the Carolingians, and were the progenitors of those vigorous Normans who later took over England, southern and eastern Scotland, Wales, Dublin and the Pale, besides creating merry hell in France and establishing kingdoms and fiefs as far away as Sicily, Greece and the Holy

I KEEP ON TRYING TO TELL YOU:
WE'RE HAVING A DANISH
PRODUCE FORTNIGHT!

19

Land. The Danes were a very great menace in the Dark Ages, frightening just about everyone to bits; their depredations, however, were largely responsible for the rapid development of feudalism and were therefore not entirely without benefit.

The first known king of all these pirates, hooligans and conquering berserkers was Gorm the Old, who ruled in Jutland around 940. Gorm might have been past his sell-by date, but he sired a memorable line of kings. His son Harald Bluetooth unified the Danes, conquered Norway, and also caused his subjects to be Christianised, for added protection. It is good to note that the Vikings in general did not let their Christianity make them into pious, milk-and-water liberals, as would be the case today, but continued to fight, rob and loot like men, which was in any case a lot more becoming for sinners.

Harald Bluetooth begat Sweyn Forkbeard, and Forkbeard begat Knud or Canute, who conquered England from Ethelred the Unready, Canute ruling both England and Denmark from 1016 till his death in 1035, when he was buried in Winchester Cathedral.

Canute's empire was soon replaced by normal medieval chaos, with wars between various Eriks, Knuds, Magnuses and their subjects, the Church and the Wends (Slavs of north and east Germany). Valdemar the Great emerged victorious in 1157, ruling in comparative peace and prosperity for some twenty-five years with the able assistance of his ally Bishop Absalon, who founded Copenhagen ('Merchants' Harbour') as a coastal fortress in 1166, set up schools, levied tax to pay for a fleet and army, and crusaded tirelessly against the Wends, spreading Denmark's territorial possessions along the north German

coast. In Valdemar's day any man who presented himself fully equipped for military service in time of war was declared a noble and thenceforth exempt from tax.

Valdemar's son, Valdemar the Victorious (1202–1241) continued his father's expansionist policy along the Baltic coast, crusading against the heathen Estonians and establishing a Danish fortress at Reval (Talinn). This Valdemar was the first to use the famous dannebrog, the Danish flag, reputedly the oldest national flag in Europe. A long period of misrule and disorder followed, in which royal power and royal finances crumbled till virtually the whole kingdom was in pawn to the neighbouring Count of Holstein. There was no king at all between 1332 and 1340.

Valdemar IV eventually got the kingdom out of hock and by 1360 on its feet again, warring with Sweden, marrying a Holsteiner and betrothing his bright young daughter, Margrethe, to the King of Norway. His most powerful enemy was the German Hanseatic League which, allied with various nobles and neighbouring states gained trading privileges all over Denmark.

On his death without male progeny, the magnates of the Rigsdag elected as King, Valdemar's infant grandson Olaf, son of Margrethe, with his mother as Regent.

Margrethe, proclaimed Queen on Olaf's death, undoubtedly took Denmark into one of its periodic climbs into the Big League principally by her Union of Kalmar in 1397, a dynastic union of Denmark, Norway and Sweden. With Norway came Iceland, Faroes, Greenland, Orkney and Shetland. With Sweden came a large part of Finland. Behind the Union lay not just the astute diplomatic skills of a brilliant woman, but the threat – which the three kingdoms were not powerful enough to resist separately – of complete

Hanseatic commercial domination and the spread of German power that went with it.

Margrethe's successor Erik began the profitable toll on all vessels passing through the Kattegat, promoted Danish trade and towns, but enraged nobles and clergy in Norway and Sweden by promoting Danes generally. He was succeeded by Christopher of Bavaria, then by the first of the present House of Oldenburg, Christian I (1448–81), since when all Danish kings with one exception have been called either Christian or Frederick, which shows a certain lack of imagination.

The first Christian spent most of his time and money defeating and bribing the nobles of Schleswig and Holstein in order to incorporate these two territories on the southern borders of Jutland into the kingdom. It was this need for funds which led him to pawn Orkney and Shetland – last remnants of the Viking empire in the British Isles – to King James III of Scots in lieu of a dowry when that monarch married a Danish princess in 1469. Apart from Christian, the early Oldenburgs were a bit too Germanic and tactless to go down a treat in Sweden, and a messy incident at the coronation of Christian II – the 'Stockholm Bloodbath', when over eighty nobles were killed – led directly to Sweden's final rebellion from the Union under Gustavus Vasa (1523).

Despite continuing wars and quarrels with nobles and clergy during these reigns, Denmark was becoming a prosperous country thanks to the commercial advantages of the Union. There were trade agreements with the Dutch and the English. Towns prospered. So did nobles, who often traded as merchants

themselves. The creation of a Lutheran state church during the reformation strengthened the monarchy, and thereafter the nobles largely ceased to oppose it, since its new-found vast estates and wealth made it a great source of goodies (as in Scotland under James VI). There was in any case general agreement that a strong monarchy was good for trade, and the way was now clear for the development of Royal absolutism.

The successors of swashbuckling Christian IV, a king who had done neither himself nor Denmark any good by entering the Thirty Years war, rebuilt the navy, and created an efficient bureaucracy. They sold off some of their excess estates to bourgeois parvenus, and followed a cautious foreign policy of attempting to keep a balance of power in the north – directed against the might of Sweden – in alliance with Russia, the Netherlands and occasionally, France.

Following the Great Northern War of 1700–21 – occasioned by ambitions of Augustus II King of Poland, Peter the Great and by the erratic genius of Swedish King Charles XII – the perennial dispute over the rightful possession of Schleswig and Holstein blossomed into new life with the rise to power of the Dukes of Holstein-Gottorp. Longer than the longest Viking Saga, this matter ran and ran interminably, until in January 1762 an insane Duke of Holstein-Gottorp suddenly became Tsar of Russia (Peter III). He immediately declared war on Denmark, which until then had been prospering quietly by profiting from the complex European wars of the mid-eighteenth century; 30,000 Danes marched to meet the Russian threat though the Russians clearly had the advantage of a fully mobilised and battle-hardened army. Fortunately, Tsar Peter was murdered

GOOD NEWS, MON BRAVE!
HER IMPERIAL MAJESTY IS DEALING
WITH THE HOLSTEIN-GOTTORP
SITUATION AT THIS VERY MOMENT.

in July 1762 and his successor, his wife, Catherine the Great, had more on her mind than Holstein-Gottorp. Denmark acquired Holstein-Gottorp in 1773.

Despite considerable efforts by the monarchy to improve their lot, the peasantry had a pretty thin time throughout this period, although that is what being a peasant is all about, of course. They were still bound by feudal strictures: no male could leave his natal village between the age of 14–40; tenants still had to labour three days a week unpaid on their lords' land. Nobles retained minor judiciary power. A system of conscription for the national army allowed landlords to send off recalcitrants to it for six years. As a result, agriculture was hardly as efficiently prosecuted as it could have been, meat and oxen being the main exports. In Norway, on the other hand, peasants had largely become yeomen farmers by the eighteenth century, prosperity flowing downwards from the profitable timber trade with Britain.

'Throughout the eighteenth century,' according to the *New Cambridge Modern History*, 'most subjects of the Danish Crown showed a complete satisfaction with absolutism . . . They congratulated themselves that the Twin Kingdoms (Denmark and Norway) were not victims of party strife, such as played itself out in Sweden from 1718 to 1772, and they compared their lot favourably with that of other monarchies where absolutism was less benevolent and enlightened than under the Oldenburgs.' But, then as now, there were liberals emerging from the wainscots to enlighten the ignorant majority. The first of these singular fellows in Denmark was a German doctor, Johann Friedrich Struensee (later Count Struensee) who crept out of the Queen's bedchamber in 1770 and, by dint of the sort of bedchamber talents that often come in useful at absolutist courts, took over the government of the more than slightly deranged King Christian VII (1766–1808). For a year and a half the good doctor had a free hand unleashing enlightened reforms including freedom of the press – always a shibboleth of the libertine. But with no popular support whatsoever, Count Struensee came to a sticky end in 1772 at the hands of enraged nobles.

Reactionaries replaced him, but the seed had been sown, and a bloodless counter-coup in 1784 ushered in a remarkable period of reforms led by a group of enlightened nobles and Crown Prince Frederick (later Frederick VI, 1808–1839) who knew what they were doing because they had already carried out the measures they proposed on their private estates. The majority of the peasants now became landowners, feudal restrictions were abolished, and lords were compensated for the loss of their privileges and land. The whole revolution was financed from Danish export profits, chiefly due to sustained and rising grain prices throughout the period 1750–1815. From such reforms sprang the high standards of Danish agriculture in the nineteenth and twentieth centuries. They made sound sense economically; politically the monarchy remained absolute – and popular – all the way through to 1849. It must be said that the Danes' use of their national revenues compares more than favourably with the appalling and stultifying waste perpetrated by absolutist regimes in other countries: Portugal and Spain, for example.

The Napoleonic wars brought an end to the long northern peace in

1801 when Nelson ('I do not see the signal') destroyed a Danish Fleet in Copenhagen harbour to prevent its falling into French hands. The Treaty of Tilsit of 1807, between Napoleon and the Tsar, made the Danes' position untenable. Fearing Russian occupation more than that of the French, they joined Napoleon's alliance, whereupon the British promptly occupied Zealand, bombarded Copenhagen and sailed away with the remainder of the Danish fleet. Thereafter the British blockade of continental Europe was extended to Denmark and Norway with particularly disastrous effects on Norway, whose timber and salt fish exports to Britain ceased, as well as her own essential imports of grain from Denmark. The sudden economic crisis and growing hunger raised a determined independence movement. Following Napoleon's defeat at the battle of Leipzig, 1813, Sweden invaded Denmark, and by the Peace of Kiel, 1814, Denmark lost Norway to Sweden though she retained Iceland, the Faroe Islands and Greenland. A pro-Danish uprising engineered by Crown Prince Christian Frederick (later King Christian VIII), Governor of Norway, got nowhere.

The Napoleonic Wars were disastrous for Denmark, who had been virtually an innocent bystander throughout. Thanks to the British, her trade, her capital and her navy were in ruins. She had lost vast territory and a considerable proportion of her population. Hamburg had replaced Copenhagen as the northern centre of international trade and finance. Rampant inflation was followed by national bankruptcy, and the crisis worsened with the universal collapse of grain prices after 1815. The period of enlightened agrarian reforms ended, and many estates went out of business. Denmark had once again left the Big League.

The nineteenth century saw the growth of the usual political parties, the urban middle class liberals merging with a growing farmers' movement in the National Liberal Party, though the monarchy retained popular support. Following the death of Christian VIII in 1848 – the Year of Revolutions, when *anciens régimes* were toppling like drunks at a wedding – his successor Frederick VII (1848–1863) abolished the autocracy and introduced a new constitution with a two-chamber parliament (Folketing and Landsting) elected by popular vote, with the king and parliamentary government sharing power. Basic laws enacted the foundations of a social democracy and welfare state far in advance of the age.

This period also brought two estimable Danish institutions. In 1844 Bishop Grundtvig founded the first of his Folk High Schools: a cross between a free university and a night school, open to all and without exams, providing excellent courses in all manner of cultural and practical subjects, and catering particularly for the rural population. As a result, the Danish farmer and rural dweller is no boor. Above all, the Folk High Schools provide knowledge of and pride in all things Danish so that the population do not idly accept trash as a substitute for a real national heritage.

Even more famous than the good bishop, his writings running second only to Holy Scripture for the number of their translations into divers tongues, Hans Christian Andersen (1805–75) was a poor boy born in Odense and scorned by his countrymen for part of his literary life, who became the world's best-known and best-loved Dane. He was an eccentric, a whimsical individual and typically Danish, his fairy stories may seem lightweight by comparison with the cultural giants of other countries, but like Lego – another great Danish contribution to civilisation – they have entered into everyone's home and been more than welcome for their fascination and endless versatility.

It was soon time for another episode of the Schleswig – Holstein serial. The nineteenth century, as well as being soft on liberalism, was also a prey to fervid nationalism. The Germans of Holstein had foolishly joined the German Confederation after 1815, the predecessor of Bismarck's Reich. The German half of the population of Schleswig soon felt a Prussian-inspired desire to do likewise. Prussia aided their rebellion during 1848–51, with the result that the Danish government agreed not to totally incorporate Schleswig into Denmark. Danish attempts to circumvent this led in 1864 to Bismarck proclaiming war on Denmark. Jutland was occupied and the Danish army, which hadn't exactly done a lot of fighting since 1720, lost 4800 men in a battle at Dybbøl Mill. As a result, Denmark lost Schleswig and Holstein, together with a third of its continental territory and about two-fifths of its population. The National Liberal government fell and a predominantly conservative period of government ensued till 1901, under King Christian XI (1863–1901). In foreign policy thereafter, a policy of neutrality was followed right through to the First World War, although the Germans forced the Danes to mine the Great Belt area between Zealand and Fünen in the First World War and, despite a non-aggression pact signed by Hitler in 1939, occupied the country from 1940.

Unfortunately lacking good allies, Denmark more than compensated for her decline in international status by her economic and social progress. Railways, industrialisation, rapidly improving farming techniques, development of harbours, ship building and trade brought in a steady flow of foreign capital. When world grain prices dived again after 1870, her farmers successfully switched to butter and bacon, with Britain their main market. Farms were efficiently organised to maximise exports, produce being standardised by successful farming co-operatives. The Danes have one big advantage, though their land is not endowed with mineral wealth or even particularly good soil: they are not seriously divided among themselves, and they are capable of working together for the good of the nation.

The twentieth century brought further democratisation, and economic problems brought about by international events outside their control: unrestricted German submarine warfare in 1917, British adoption of a policy of Imperial preference in the 1930s. The Versailles Peace settlement after the First World War returned parts of Schleswig where the Danish population showed by plebiscite that they didn't want to remain in Germany. German occupation in the Second World War left a coalition government intact and the Royal Family in residence, though the government had to toe the line on policy matters: they joined Hitler's Anti-Comintern Pact of 1941 and a Danish volunteer corps was raised to fight in the USSR. Passive resistance and active sabotage

of German army activities became a national pastime for young and old. When Jews were ordered by Nazi decree to wear yellow stars, the whole population including the King, took to wearing them while Jews were quietly shipped out to safety in Sweden. German defeats in the USSR together with increasing dissatisfaction with wartime shortages led to increased resistance, as a result of which in 1943 the Germans terminated Danish sovereignty and installed a Reichskommissioner. The Danes took to wearing woollen hats knitted in RAF roundel patterns.

Since the Second World War, Denmark has not had an easy ride economically, owing to international slumps and crises such as the oil crisis of 1974. Her ingenuity, common sense, drastic taxation and some harsh austerity measures have carried her through, together with a social security scene that caters for everyone from womb to tomb. By 1945, neutrality was clearly discredited as a foreign policy: she joined NATO in 1949, EFTA in 1959, and the EEC in 1973. Proportional representation and the abolition of the Landsting (Upper House) in 1953 have resulted in a proliferation of political parties and a long series of coalition and minority governments unable to maintain themselves in power for very long. There is, perhaps, a certain Socialist anaemia, a certain prevalent lack of inspiration, which contrasts with the more dashing Danish periods of the past, but if History has a message for Denmark it is that, like a cork in the Kattegat, she will always bob up again.

FRANCE

France is the largest and richest country in Western Europe, and the French have, as a result, always been insufferably superior. Even in the Ice Ages, 25,000 years ago, the prehistoric inhabitants were off to a cultural lead on the walls of caves like that at Lascaux, whilst the rest of Europe was still trying to figure out how to light a fire. The Ancient Greeks, always pretty keen on culture, came here 2,500 years ago, founding Marseilles. Then there were the Iron Age Celts, fierce, brave Gauls like Vercingetorix, who finished up as part of Julius Caesar's triumphal procession through the teeming streets of Rome in 45 BC. The French, of course, had to be conquered by someone who was both a military and a literary genius. It took the legions twelve years of hard fighting, revolts and bloody reprisals before the work was done, but three hundred years of civilisation followed, in which the Romans organised

HE SAYS REPRESENTATIONAL ART HAS HAD ITS DAY.

the country in provinces, built roads and cities, developed agriculture and commerce.

When the Western Roman Empire collapsed in the fifth century, its structures and essentials were preserved in France by the Roman Church.

The survival of the West was the work of the Church, of such men as Pope Gregory the Great. They observed what was happening and made their choice of men. Charles of the House of Pepin, Carolus Magnus, Charlemagne, became King of the Franks in 768, and the Church had found her champion. He was an immense barbarian chief, with eight wives, despotic, a militant Christian. He could kill a man with one blow of his club, and was proud of it. In forty-six years of campaigns against the Lombards, Saxons, Byzantines and Umayyads he established a Frankish Empire across France, Germany and Italy. On Christmas Day 800, Pope Leo III – whom Charlemagne had recently rescued from well-substantiated charges of murder, adultery, simony and perjury – crowned him Roman Emperor in Rome. He learned to read and make his mark, and gathered Italian and Anglo-Saxon scholars to his court. He was a legendary figure then and for hundreds of years to come, his ideal of a Christian Empire of Europe remaining a vital international concept for a thousand years, and in a debilitated form it is alive yet in the European Community.

However, the Empire broke up in the innumerable wars of Charlemagne's descendants. Danish Vikings sailed up the great rivers to burn and loot Amiens, Paris, Orleans and countless lesser places. Monks and nobles fled before them. In 911, King Charles the Simple granted Jarl Rollo his own land for Norse settlement – Normandy – with dire results for France over the following 500 years.

The last Carolingian, Louis V, died in 987, whereupon two ambitious Churchmen persuaded the magnates to elect Hugh Capet, first of a singular and tenacious dynasty that lasted till the nineteenth century. For the Capets, the chief menace was the growing power of the independent and efficiently organised Duchy of Normandy, especially after 1066, when Duke William conquered England. The resulting fusion of the vigorous, ruthless Norman aristocracy with Anglo-Saxon England meant that France wasn't going to lack for an ambitious predator on her western flank. The Capets did what they could, took advantage of any weakness that came their way – such as the Stephen versus Matilda struggle – but by mid-twelfth century, the English King Henry II ruled one of the strongest monarchies in Europe, stretching from the Tweed to the Pyrenees and including half of France. When Henry's rebellious sons proved a thorn in his flesh, Philip Augustus (1180–1223) played them for all he was worth, befriending Richard and John, then when Richard became King and disappeared on the Third Crusade, playing John against his brother and arranging for Richard's incarceration in Austria on his way home from the Holy Land. In 1199, Richard was shot dead at the siege of a minor castle by a French crossbowman. In 1214, at the Battle of Bouvines, the luckless King John was driven from France while Philip's armies pressed into Normandy, Brittany, Anjou and the rest of the English monarch's possessions. Philip was the first of the Capets to emerge from local feudal conflicts onto the European stage. He further profited from the Fourth Crusade, which took troublesome barons off his back to plunder Constantinople, and from the Albigensian Crusade – stamping out heretics and social revolution in the Mediterranean south – which increased his control in that area and resulted in new ideas and Gothic architecture coming north.

It was now time for the best of the Middle Ages: chivalry, troubadours, St Bernard, Abelard, Aquinas, the University of Paris, Gothic cathedrals and Villhardouin's *Chronicles*. The hour called forth the man – as happens with irritating inevitability in French history. King Louis IX, St Louis, was far and away the most attractive of the Capets – admittedly not an attractive bunch at their best – a perfect mirror of chivalry, pious but charming with it: hardly a common type in modern times. More to the point, he was an absolutist. He succeeded to the throne as a minor at a time of crisis. Whilst his mother remained Regent, he put down English-inspired baronial revolts and went on the Seventh Crusade. After her death in 1253, he became the Great Justiciary, extending royal justice throughout the realm, abolishing trial by combat, establishing a single currency, correcting incompetence and malpractice. He made peace with his neighbours Henry III of England and James, King of Aragon. He died on the Eighth Crusade, fighting before Tunis (1270).

From this time on, the Capets considered themselves far enough up the ladder to indulge from time to time their weakness for silly foreign wars, chiefly in Italy and Flanders. In both regions, there were famous massacres of Frenchmen: the Sicilian Vespers, 1282, caused the French King's uncle, Charles of Anjou, who ruled there, to eat his own sceptre in rage. A similar massacre of obnoxious Frenchmen, the 'Bruges Matins', took place during the following reign of Philip the Fair (1302) at the behest of Guy, Count of Flanders, a chum of Edward I of England. It was Philip the Fair, early in the 14th century, strapped for cash to pay for the burgeoning royal bureaucracy, who summoned the first Estates General, in which each of the three estates – clergy, nobles and commons – met separately, though the first two had quite a lot in common, both being exempt from taxation.

Baronial reaction against increasing royal power occupied the reigns of Philip's sons with chaos, famine, unsuccessful wars, persecutions of Jews, wholesale slaughter of lepers and royal suppression of the Knights Templar – to get cash. The original Capets were succeeded by the Valois branch just in time for the start of the Hundred Years War with England (1337–1453). This was basically a trade war by the Flemings (Belgians) and English, enlivened by Edward III's cheeky claim to the French throne and a general English desire for booty. The Valois and their nobles were mainly prats playing at chivalry, whilst the English were professional soldiers, their tactical skills, discipline, archers and small cannon seeing off the French knights at such fabled encounters as Crécy, 1346. The Black Death stalked the countryside. More Jews were slaughtered. Flagellants ate nails and fire. French barons with a desire to rise, or a grudge to pay off, contacted the English and offered their services. At the Battle of Poitiers, 1356, the French King John the Good, was captured and shipped to London where he lived a life of gilded ease. (He was nicknamed Good not on account of any moral superiority but because he liked a good time.) Later, he was ransomed by French taxpayers for three million gold crowns. There is no doubt that the English and Belgians knew how to turn an honest bob or two from the French during this period.

Froissart, in his chronicles of this age, tells of the hatred felt for the militarily incompetent nobility. A Parisian, Etienne Marcel, organised the citizens and put forward democratic demands to the Estates with the aid of the Bishop of Laon. Peasants, mercilessly screwed for cash to ransom worthless nobles, rose in rebellion – the 'Jacquerie'. But these were all brutally suppressed. When King John the Good was released from captivity in London, he proceeded to make further blunders, idiotically gave away the Duchy of Burgundy to his son Philip the Bold, then, on learning that another son had escaped from England having previously given his word to remain there as a hostage, he returned voluntarily to his gilded cage across the Channel, where he died in 1364, during the chivalric festivities laid on by the English to greet his return. 'Great Companies' of unemployed soldiery roamed and harried the land during this period of peace.

The next king, Charles V, was a weakling, not deluded by visions of knightly chivalry. Nor was his excellent subordinate Bertrand du Guesclin, a Breton knight, who now began to turn the tables on the English by avoiding pitched battles and depriving them of material support. Again, the hour called forth the man. By 1375, English possessions had shrunk to little more than the Calais bridgehead, Brest, Bayeaux and Bayonne, and the French were raiding the

English coast. Edward III and his equally beligerent son, the Black Prince, died. Yet Charles was no sooner quit of them than he succeeded in creating as big a menace on his eastern and northern borders by marrying his brother Philip the Bold to the heiress of Flanders, recreating a Lotharingia for the next hundred years.

His successor, Charles VI (1380–1427), proved to be remarkably inept. His uncles, the Dukes of Burgundy, Anjou, Berry and Bourbon, got rapidly out of hand, pausing only now and then to suppress hopeless peasant Jacqueries. Countless lesser spats developed into a major political quarrel between the Burgundians, who controlled Flanders and looked for an English alliance, and the King's younger brother Louis of Orleans. Burgundy murdered Orleans in 1407. Louis's supporters controlled the King and the Dauphin, his heir, and were known as Armagnacs. Between them, the two groups tore France apart. Then in stepped young, handsome Henry V, King of England, with his little army, keen to win renown for the upstart House of Lancaster. They smashed an Armagnac host at the Battle of Agincourt, 1415, and by the Treaty of Troyes (1422) Henry became Regent and heir of France, marrying the King's daughter.

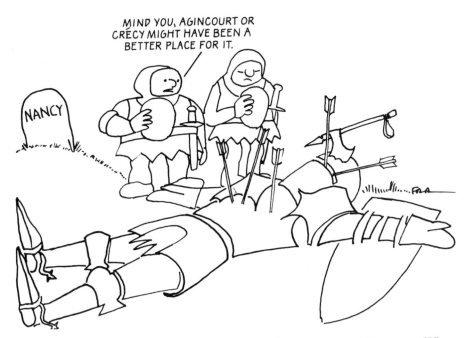

The English took Brittany, Normandy, Maine, Champagne and Guyenne. When Charles died the infant Henry VI of England was proclaimed his successor. The Dauphin Charles, a weakling, was left with a Vichy-type state, derisively known as the 'Kingdom of Bourges' after its capital. It seemed only a matter of a short time till the English had it all.

This appalling time for France was also paradoxically a period of high culture, of *Les Très Riches Heures* of the Duc du Berry and of growing – and genuine – nationalism. Once again, the hour called forth a champion: a seventeen-year-old maiden from Lorraine, the incomparable Joan of Arc. She turned the English around almost single-handedly, though like most great leaders she seemed to personify feelings that lay deep within the inarticulate masses, shaming the sophisticated and cynical nobility. She did more than defeat the English: she created French patriotism. And for her trouble, the English burned her as a 'witch' (1431). By 1453, the English had lost the lot except Calais and the Channel Islands, and the Hundred Years War was over.

There remained the menace of Burgundy, which now extended under the ambitious Duke Charles the Rash from Holland to Savoy, with one gap, Lorraine, which Charles aimed to fill. To prevent this, the spider-like Louis XI (1461–83) intrigued and bribed and plotted interminably. In 1477 the bold Charles was killed at the Battle of Nancy and Burgundian power was at an end. Part of the duchy reverted to Louis, but the main parts, including Flanders – much to Louis' chagrin – went to the Habsburgs. Louis, a more sinister version of Henry Tudor, his contemporary, was a distinctly non-feudal type, unpopular with his nobles for employing jumped-up nobodies in his administration, interested in developing industry, trade and communications. Endlessly suspicious – not without reason – he spent his free time building Plessis les Tours, a château with an exceptionally elaborate security system, and when he had finished it he died.

For the next 300 years, the Habsburgs, elevated by clever marriages from Germanic obscurity to dominion over most of the known and unknown world by the time of the Emperor Charles V (1519–55), proved an even greater menace than the English. Not only did they control almost all the surrounding territory, but they also had the treasure of the New World to help finance their efforts. Little wonder that French kings of these centuries were distinctly nervous types. Nor did overmighty French nobles disappear with the waning of feudal times: they remained a constant and unpredictable threat till the reign of Louis XIV. As elsewhere, the Reformation gave everyone extra reasons for killing and betraying his neighbours during wars, massacres and assassinations in the name of religion.

Despite their difficulties, however, French kings generally managed through-out to be provocative and unattractive. Charles VIII, Louis XII and Francis I – a big, flashy, superficial contemporary of big, flashy, superficial Henry VIII – all campaigned in pursuit of chimera in Italy, till the Habsburgs saw them off. The Renaissance came north with them, especially Niccolò Machiavelli the Florentine writer on political opportunism. Francis was a centralising absolutist with a brilliant court. These three were succeeded by a gloomy religious bigot, Henry II (1547–59), who kicked off a long period of religious civil wars. The Guise family – militant Catholics – led by the Duc de Guise, tended to take over everything, including Scotland, and it was a Duc de Guise who finally drove the English out of Calais. Opposition to them centred on the rival family of the Duc de Bourbon, and on the Calvinist Huguenots. These power groups fought and murdered their way through the reigns of Henry's three sons: Francis II, sickly adolescent husband of Mary Queen of Scots; Charles IX, in whose reign the Massacre of St Bartholomew's Day occurred (1572); and the inept and scandalous homosexual Henry III, who started off as elective King of Poland and ran away from there to Italy to escape a fate worse than death at the hands of the brutal Poles. In all, there were nine civil wars involving the Guises, the Bourbons and the Huguenots. It was in the last of these – the War of the Three Henries – that Henry III, the last of the Valois, was assassinated. And not before time.

France was exhausted, but a party of moderates had been forming, prepared to give tolerance a try. The hour produced the man: Henry, King of Navarre, a Bourbon but a Protestant, and sole surviving heir to the throne. He had to fight his way to it, but he secured it with a classic compromise that gained him the support of all moderates: he became a Catholic. 'Paris is worth a mass' was his catchphrase. Reconciliation, pacification and prosperity were his aims. His Edict of Nantes (1598) granted Protestants freedom of worship, unrestricted career opportunities, and the right to maintain their own military strongholds. Arguably, it created a state within the state, but France was no stranger to these. The King's finance minister, Sully, created prosperity, reformed the tax system

HE'S NOT EXACTLY
LECH WALENSKA
IS HE?

– even if the non-tax-paying nobles failed to notice – and beefed up agricultural production, while Henry held back the Habsburgs. Quebec was founded 1608. Henry was, and remains, a popular king: benevolent, capable, an absolutist and a womaniser. He was certainly different from his predecessor, but he too was assassinated, in 1610, by Ravaillac, a maniac. There were a lot of them about.

Louis XIII's reign (1610–43) was the age of Cardinal Richelieu, not the first great churchman to devote his energies and talents to making French kings strong. Louis was only eight when his father was stabbed, and once again there were rebellions by both nobles and Huguenots. Not without justification, Richelieu's aims were 'to ruin the Huguenots and bring down the pride of the nobility' and he was thoroughly successful. Following the siege of La Rochelle (1627), the Huguenots lost their fortresses and most of their privileges. Next the Cardinal turned on the nobles: he plotted, razed castles, beheaded opponents, built up a centralised autocracy with a middle-class civil service, his *intendants* were dispatched throughout the country to govern provinces efficiently behind the glitter of their noble governors. Richelieu was lucky as well as clever. Germany – with the involvement of Spaniards, Danes and Swedes – was tearing itself apart with the horrific Thirty Years War, drastically weakening the Habsburgs; and that was due as much to the Cardinal's masterly diplomacy as to the feats of arms of such titans as Gustavus Adolphus.

And so to Louis XIV, the Sun King, 'the most resplendent monarch ever', who, served at various stages by brilliant ministers – Mazarin, Fouquet, Colbert – triumphed with their aid over both the German and Spanish Habsburgs, and over the rebellious nobles of the Fronde risings. He established a dazzling

absolutism, which he exercised from the vast and vulgar palace he built for himself at Versailles. He desired and obtained grandeur, huge buildings, territorial expansion. His army was reformed by Louvois, his siege techniques and fortifications perfected by Vauban. He revoked the Edict of Nantes and lost 250 000 industrious Huguenot subjects – who took their skills abroad – without a qualm. He waged thirty-one years of war, placed his grandson on the throne of the Habsburgs' Spanish Empire and generally made his enemies look rather *passé*. He made mistakes – his attack on the Netherlands created an implacable enemy in William of Orange – but he solved the longest running of all France's problems by reducing his own nobles to the role of gilded, powdered popinjays required by a uniquely French form of blackmail to dance attendance on him at Versailles, to watch him pirouetting about, eating huge meals or sitting on his potty. The rest of Europe, instead of sitting back and laughing, ran to ape it all; French manners, language, cuisine, fashions, architecture became without question the mode at every semi-civilised court from Whitehall to Moscow. Such was the genius of Louis XIV.

He was a hard act to follow. His son and his grandson had predeceased him when he died in 1715. Louis XV, his great grandson, was a frivolous idler in a world of frivolous idlers, and it was downhill all the way. No one, then or since, completely understood the finances of a show like Louis XIV's, but whoever paid for Versailles and the thirty-one years of warfare – including some heavy defeats by Marlborough and the Habsburg general Prince Eugene – it certainly wasn't the nobles or clergy. Although Louis had started to levy the *vingtieme* in the 1690s to help meet the cost of war, both the nobility and clergy remained tax-exempt.

In past centuries the nobles, no matter how insufferable, had at least lived in the countryside surrounded by their peasants, and the local chateau had been a continuing source of employment, gossip, pain, war, misery, even at times enjoyment and benefit. Not all nobles were monstrous. The point however, is that the French, unlike less vigorous peoples, will put up with warfare, persecution, feudalism and wanton exploitation but they will not tolerate *boredom* indefinitely. When all their aristocrats – or all who wished to be thought anything other than bumpkins – went off to swan around Versailles, it wasn't the resulting idleness, luxury and moral turpitude that got up the people's noses, it was the boredom. The only possible justification for a noble caste in a post-feudal era is that its members provide show, spark, *bon ton*, gossip, kicks up the backside for otherwise inward-looking rural communities. When they cease for whatever reason to perform this vital function their number is up – as happened later in Ireland and Russia. And the French, irritating as ever, were the first to demonstrate this great principle.

There were other factors. One was the largely pointless wars of Louis XV (War of Polish Succession, War of Austrian Succession, Seven Years War) which ended with the total loss of France's overseas empire (Louisiana, India, Canada) and the corresponding rise of Britain to Great Power status. A second was the financial crisis which these wars precipitated – the country was bankrupt by the time of poor Louis XVI (1774–93). A third was the steadily rising population – French peasants were better off than peasants elsewhere (always an ingredient for revolution). Yet another was the radical, libertarian philosophers of the period – Diderot, Montesquieu, Voltaire, Rousseau – whose ideas became highly fashionable and must to an unknown extent have undermined the confidence of the frivolous idlers. There was also the American War of Independence, with French volunteers such as the Marquis de Lafayette arriving back in France full of enthusiasm for Liberty. And of course, there was the dear old rising bourgeoisie, prosperous but socially and politically out in the dark. But greater than all these was boredom.

When the collapse came, it came like the rot-infested timbers of an old mansion collapsing: everyone knew something was going to happen but no one expected it to go as it did, first one floor then another, and finally the whole crumbling tatty edifice collapsing in a great heap of old rubbish.

Suddenly it was time for the French Revolution, the strident Assemblies, the dithering and rabble-rousing, the Girondins and Jacobins, men such as Robespierre, Marat, Mirabeau and all the other fanatics who sprang nimbly like rats from nooks and crannies in that collapsing house. Suffice to say they all emerged and had their day, including the members of the Committee of Public Safety with their Reign of Terror and their 'Representatives on Mission' touring the country liquidating opponents and suspects. They guillotined Louis and God knows how many tens of thousands of others. 'O Liberty! What crimes are committed in thy name!' They abolished Christianity and set up – with supreme

irony – the Worship of Reason. They began a new epoch and a new Revolutionary calendar, with Saints' days abolished and festivals in honour of, for example, the Pig and the Dungheap. It was all a hideous, unplanned slide into madness, but it certainly stopped the boredom. From every corner of France, from every class and condition of men and women, a great new popular spirit was unleashed, the spirit of a Revolutionary nation in arms, the spirit of 'La Marseillaise'. They trampled their old ruins underfoot, and marched off singing to spread Liberty, Equality and Fraternity throughout Europe.

The neighbours didn't like it. They had looked on with glee and approval while the French tore down their own mansion, but now that they were coming to demolish other people's ancient piles it could mean only one thing: war. Liberty can win revolutions but it cannot win wars. Wars need armies. Armies need generals. And, as every Roman knew, general and emperor are the same word. So the French finished their Revolution by having an Emperor, Napoleon Bonaparte, instead of a King, Louis Capet.

As Emperors go, he was certainly a very inspiring one. He codified the laws – as every emperor since the time of Hammurabi has done. He exercised a firm hand, which everyone appreciated after all the Revolutionary fervour. He waged continual war, dominated Europe, scattered his family and friends all across the continent like festive glitter: three kings, a queen, a grand duchess and lots of new dukes, marquesses and marshals. All very egalitarian, in a French sort of way. He had unique style, which the French relished, and the sartorial fashions were quite superb. The English hated him. After the Battle of Trafalgar (1805) they set about strangling him by an exceptionally effective commercial blockade. His effect upon every European country was immense and drastic, galvanising sudden political change, scientific advance, administrative efficiency, political union: above all by demonstrating to the whole of Europe, and thence to the world, what could be done by activating the masses. Without doubt it was the dawn of a new age, an age that led via revolutions, mass politics and the gutter press to Hitler and Stalin. Once again, the French had shown the way.

Eventually, Napoleon's wars became too big a burden: the Peninsular War – a unique and unlikely combination of British military skill and Portuguese and Spanish popular uprising – and the Moscow campaign of 1812. The British, the Spanish, the Russians and the Prussians closed in, slowly, and his empire vanished. A Chamber of Deputies thronging with Royalists restored the Bourbon monarchy in the person of Louis XVIII. His minister, the Duc de Richelieu skilfully prevented a White Terror. The war-weary French seemed perfectly content.

To this day the French themselves have not made up their minds about that greatest and first of Revolutions. It was certainly the most cataclysmic event in Europe since the Thirty Years War, and we continue to live with its consequences. By it, France lost a well-balanced self-assurance, a noble

grandeur. As for Napoleon, it is almost as if he himself felt this, and laboured mightily to replace the loss by his breathtaking achievements. In the nineteenth and twentieth centuries, despite bold colonial exploits in North Africa and Indo-China, despite the gallant efforts of Napoleon III and General de Gaulle, it was clear that something had gone out of France that did not return, as if God had withdrawn his long-suffering Grace with the coming of the Age of Reason. Three terrible wars – the Franco-Prussian War and two World Wars – prove it. And so do the politics in between: like an ageing roué, France since 1815 has tried everything without satisfaction: five republics, a second empire, several revolutions and communes, various sorts of king, more constitutions than was good for her, provisional governments, putsches and failed coups by Bourbonists, Orleanists, Bonapartists and crooks of more humble origin, direct rule by Nazis and an État Français.

Charles X (1824–30), the last reigning Bourbon was a reactionary in a period of rapidly developing industrial and scientific progress. He was replaced by Louis-Philippe, of the Orleanist branch of the dynasty, son of a notorious Jacobin and pervert, Philippe Egalité, Duc d'Orleans. He played the part required of him as a 'Citizen King', strolling around Paris with an umbrella, while opposition gathered around him from a variety of quarters, including the new Socialists. The Industrial Revolution was in full swing with the attendant unsatisfactory working and living conditions. There were riots, risings, railways and romantics. And boredom with Louis-Philippe and his old umbrella. The King and Queen left hastily for England, appropriately as Mr and Mrs Smith, when the 'Year of Revolutions' (1848) dawned. A provisional government of Socialists set about solving everyone's problems with naïve idealism. Fresh insurrections were suppressed by one General Cavaignac, who shot the Archbishop of Paris as well as a number of other people. When the constitution makers set up a presidential election, an unexpected candidate won: Louis Napoleon, nephew of the late, great Emperor. It did not take him long thereafter – introducing a modern flair for carefully orchestrated whistle-stop railway tours and plebiscites – to do for the Second Republic what his distinguished predecessor had done for the First.

The Second Empire of Napoleon III (1852–70) – whatever happened to Napoleon II – was an interesting, vibrant period of rapid commercial expansion, material prosperity, cultural and architectural exuberance, including Baron Haussmann's ambitious rebuilding of Paris. Even among such luminaries as Flaubert, Baudelaire, the Impressionists and Offenbach, Napoleon himself, though he never quite lost the air of an adventurous trickster was a person of enigmatic but real talent, a populist with a sure touch for appeals to the people. His empire was basically peaceful – even allowing for foreign campaigns in Italy, Vietnam, Syria, China and Mexico – and became less dictatorial as it went on: there was a parliamentary revival, a free and vigorous press, legal trade unions and strikes. By 1869 France had become virtually a constitutional monarchy. But Napoleon had reckoned without the remorseless rise of modern Germany. In the short, brutal Franco-Prussian War of 1870, the bourgeois glamour and Napoleonic gallantry shot to hell by Prussian artillery in a sinister triumph of

NO I'M NOT
SALVADOR BLOODY DALI.

efficiency. The King of Prussia was proclaimed German Emperor at Versailles, and with appalling Teutonic tactlessness, the victorious German army paraded in full fig – not for the last time – down the Champs-Elysées. By a humiliating peace treaty, the French lost Alsace and Lorraine, and promised to pay 5 million francs, which, thanks to Napoleon III's economic miracle, they did by 1873. It is hardly surprising that after the First World War similar conditions were imposed on the Germans.

Everyone expected a Bourbon restoration, but it came to nothing; the claimant, the Comte de Chambord, insisting with almost inconceivable pettiness that the Bourbon flag replace the tricolour. A Third Republic came into existence that no one wanted and few bothered to support. It produced fifty prime ministers in less than fifty years, mainly mediocrities or worse. Scandals and financial swindles were regular. The aptly named President Grévy, for example, had to resign when his son-in-law was caught making a fortune from the Honours List. The spark left politics and went into trade, industry, colonies, trade unions, socialism, artistic and intellectual pursuits – the febrile spawn of a brilliant but troubled nation. Until his departure from office in 1890, Bismarck did all he could to divert French energies into faraway colonies, away from the Rhine, and to cause conflicts with Britain. But in this at least Germany was eventually thwarted: Delcassé, one of the few decent ministers of this period, and Edward VII, an unlikely candidate for international greatness, brought about an unexpected Entente Cordiale between very old enemies.

France was not in a fit state morally, politically or militarily for the horrors of modern war. Her troops in 1914 went into action in red trousers. Morale faltered many time during those four years. Following the monstrous bloodshed around Verdun (1916) for example, 30 000 mutineers were dealt with by Pétain. One and a half million Frenchmen died.

The Treaty of Versailles, 1919, by which the French sought to create security for their declining population satisfied no-one. Marshal Foch described it accurately at the time as a twenty-year truce. The twenty years were characterised by political ineptitude, industrial unrest and seedy scandals. Nobody loved the Republic. Communism grew: so did Fascism. Demands for reparations were followed by illusory guarantees of European peace: a number of treaties known as the Pact of Locarno (1925) followed by the Kellogg Pact (1928). Militarily, the ineptitude produced the Maginot Line, which left a 250 mile gap for Belgium to defend – although the Belgians had reverted to neutrality by 1936. In the same year the French missed the opportunity of crushing Hitler's adventurism when he remilitarised the Rhineland using cardboard tanks and token troops. Appeasement was preferred. A brittle cultural brilliance – Matisse, Malraux, René Clair and Maurice Chevalier – continued to attract a myriad fluttering butterflies and moths.

It was inevitable that when France was invaded by the Wehrmacht in 1940 she collapsed. Hitler had observed her weakness, both political and military, and forced his generals to strike. The Fuhrer's surrender terms were deliberately moderate: the Germans occupied the north west, leaving the Vichy régime, under the First World War hero Marshal Pétain, in control of the remainder. It is easy to denounce Pétain's État Français with its slogan 'Work, Family, Fatherland' in place of 'Liberty, Equality, Fraternity' as collaborationist. Yet Liberty, Equality and Fraternity had produced the France of 1939.

It is also easy to mock the lonely figure in refugee London who now took it upon himself to lift the tawdry standard of France out of the mud. The hour produced the man, and he was virtually alone. Charles de Gaulle was the greatest patriot the French had produced for a very long time. He had few advantages and very little help from his Allies, some of whom regarded him throughout as a nuisance, touchy and vain. But the Free French, like the General himself, seemed almost to emerge from earlier, grander centuries. Overcoming enormous obstacles placed in his path by the Allies, the Germans and the Communists, he entered Paris in triumph in August 1944, having dodged into France on the heels of the D-Day landings. He faced some huge difficulties: hunger, poverty, massive destruction, the effects of German deportations, the low morale of a people who had had to live with the Nazis for four years: some by resistance, some by collaboration, most by *attentisme* (playing it by ear). A grim period of revenge, of paying off old scores followed, unavoidable in a land of bitterness.

Not since the time of Joan of Arc had France stood in such need of rehabilitation. De Gaulle rebuilt the country, with generous help from the USA. And even while deeply immersed in his labours, he struggled to preserve his country's place among the Great Powers – for him the key to French rebirth.

When he had made it safe, his many critics emerged from the shadows and accused him of preferring glory to welfare. He resigned the presidency only two months after it was conferred on him in 1946.

The Fourth Republic was as unstable and lacking in popular support as its predecessor, but a lot less seedy. There *was* a new spirit. The economist Jean Monet proposed the plan which led to the European Coal & Steel Community in 1951, which in turn led to the Treaty of Rome and, in 1957, the founding of the EEC. It was the colonial crisis that toppled the Republic, not lack of application. The Battle of Dien Bien Phu (1954) marked the end of French control in Indo-China. In 1954 they were out of Morocco, then Tunisia. The Algeria crisis (1956–61) was the most serious because of the hundreds of thousands of French settlers who had been there for generations. It was also regarded by the army as a place they could not give up without dishonour. The resulting Algerian civil war roused intense passions, and the government, fearing its spread to mainland France, recalled the General, then aged sixty-seven, as the only man in France likely to be able to deal with it.

First he demanded, and received, full powers, including presidential control of the government, thereby giving French politics a stability it had lacked since 1870. With great courage he granted Algerian independence – exactly what many of his supporters had wanted him in power to prevent. For the next two years he went in daily danger of assassination from embittered army men and ex-colonists. But he had the people behind him, and retained their support by elaborate TV appearances and tours reminiscent of Napoleon III. The General knew what had made the best of French kings effective: a firm hand, a determination to keep France great, and popular appeal. He would not have been out of place in any of the finer pages of her rich history. The present Fifth Republic is his legacy.

VIVE LE LUNCH LIBRE.

Germany

'The whole life of the Germans,' wrote the ubiquitous Caesar, 'is spent in hunting and the practice of war.' He was lucky the Germans were keen on hunting, and internecine strife. He pushed Rome's frontier to the Rhine, but when the Emperor Augustus tried pushing it to the Elbe, he suffered one of the greatest Roman defeats ever, when three legions commanded by Publius Quintilius Varus were ambushed and annihilated, AD 6, at the Battle of the Teutoburgerwald. Their leader on this famous occasion was Herman, Arminius, whose enormous statue dominates the Teutoburgerwald to this very day. He has not been forgotten.

In Central Europe the kingdoms of the Dark Ages – of the Franks, Allemans, Goths, Saxons, etc. – developed from coalescing tribes. By 810, Charlemagne's Frankish Empire contained most of the Germans – he spent thirty years adding the Saxons. His capital was at Aachen. His empire was intended to be not a unitary state, but a Christian commonwealth with necessary regulations about the prices of basic commodities, repair of roads, taxes and a common currency.

His successors proved inadequate in the face of disorder and break-up resulting in a bewildering collection of kingdoms ruled by mysterious Dark Age characters with undignified nicknames – Charles the Bald and Louis the Stammerer to name but two. But the ideal of a Holy Roman German Empire remained alive thanks to popes using the award of what had become an empty title to persuade various Carolingians to rescue them from their Italian involvements.

The tenth and eleventh centuries, however, saw the growth of population and towns, forest giving way to fields. Towns attracted the vigorous and enterprising, and became islands of safety and wealth. They obtained charters of freedom by revolt or by purchase, especially during the Crusades when barons and princes needed to raise cash. Frederick Barborossa (1152–1190) was your archetypal great and good German Emperor of the high Middle Ages, reviving the Empire in all its considerable glory. But basically his power depended on conciliating the magnates whose ever-growing independence was the inevitable price Frederick and his successors paid for continuing involvement in Italy.

Subsequent Emperors had less and less control, and a restructured Electoral College took bribes from such rich foreigners as Richard of Cornwall and Alfonso X of Castille for the award of what was becoming an empty title. The Teutonic Knights, slung out of Syria by the Turks, pushed into heathen Prussia, building great castles and forest towns. Peasants, burghers and nobles swarmed after them. An obscure Swabian, Count Rudolf of Habsburg was elected in

1273, and Rudolf promptly began the Habsburgs' tortuous rise to power by annexing Bohemia. Another ambitious house were the Luxemburgs, but like the Empire itself they were curious anachronisms, trying hard to exercise an imperial order north and south of the Alps which had failed to exist. Robber barons proliferated, preying on commerce and the undefended countryside. The Black Death (1347–50), reduced the population by a third, and recurred every decade to prevent recovery. Trade fell off. Cities stopped expanding. Wages rose but food prices outstripped them. It was God's anger, they said. Earthquakes shook the Rhineland. Jews were persecuted and expelled. In the west Burgundy absorbed imperial fiefs; in the east, Poland smashed the Teutonic Knights. By the close of the Middle Ages, Germany was a jigsaw of sixty-six free cities, 240 states, several hundred free imperial knights, each of them absolute monarchs of their minute fiefs. Below the seven Electors, there were fifty ecclesiastical and thirty lay princes, usually at war with each other. The peasantry was in decline and serfdom was making a comeback, particularly in the east, but even in south and central Germany the magnates were encroaching more and more on the peasantry, restricting their hunting rights, subjecting them to military service, taxing ever more efficiently as Roman Law replaced the ancient custom of the tribe. The German peasants did not take this vigorous growth of tyranny passively, but rose in murderous revolts under their Peasants' Shoe Banner, some anti-clerical, some radical and socialist. In the three decades before Luther, there were at least eleven serious peasant revolts. Heretics such as the Hussites and even scholars such as William of Ockham attacked the power and corruption of the papacy and the Church. Harvests were bad. Syphilis arrived. The world was widely expected to end in 1500. Shedding the yoke of anarchy and oppression, thousands fled into the forests or flocked to hear visionaries such as the shepherd Hans Böhem denounce idle, corrupt popes, clergy and nobles and advocate the abolition of taxes and the common freedom of forest and water. Not surprisingly, Böhem was burned at the stake. Towns alone remained, within their walls, havens of prosperous capitalism, literacy, craftsmanship and scholarship. Booksellers flourished there. Dürer, the great German artist, was born in Nürnberg in 1471.

The last Emperor crowned in Rome was the Habsburg, Frederick III (1440–93), and when Charles the Rash, Duke of Burgundy, and ruler of some of the choicest parts of Europe was killed at the Battle of Nancy (1477), Frederick's son Maximilian, betrothed to Charles' heiress Mary, succeeded him.

Maximilian himself, a tall, bold, hawk-nosed, young man obsessed with chivalry and tournaments, used his new wealth to play the Caesar, and is probably best commemorated by Dürer's triumphal arch. The arch was constructed of paper, and paper in the form of marriage contracts was the Habsburg's strongest card. It was due to their marriage alliances with the Spanish royal house that Maximilian's grandson Charles, became King of Spain and all its New World territories in 1516. Spanish gold helped the German Electors choose him as Maximilian's successor as Holy Roman Emperor in 1519 while still only nineteen.

Meanwhile, however, back at the Church, Luther had nailed up his Ninety-Five Theses protesting against the sale of Papal Indulgences – or Passports to Heaven, as Tetzel, the monk in charge of the marketing operation called them. He was working for the Archbishop of Magdeburg, who needed the money because he had just bought another archbishopric, Mainz, from Pope Leo X for 29,000 Rhenish florins.

Luther's purely religious protest rapidly became the focus for all the pent-up peasant resentment and desperation in Germany – much to Luther's alarm – and the sequel serves to remind us that Germany, not France or Russia, has long been the birthplace of true Socialist revolution. A hundred thousand peasant rebels died fighting against 'princes, lords and priests' in the Great Peasant War of 1524, and over a thousand monasteries and castles were razed. Luther, rather sickeningly, denounced it all whilst he hid safely with the Elector of Saxony throughout the action. Emperor Charles, with an empire stretching from Hungary to the Phillipines, had more than enough on his plate to worry about, including the Turkish advance into eastern Europe. He tried, as champion of the Catholic church, to smash the Protestants – the peasants were smashed by the nobles – but before retiring to a Spanish monastery he had to put up with the splitting of Germany into Lutheran and Catholic camps. The Peace of Augsburg (1555) enunciated the famous principle: *Cujus regio ejus religio*

— a state's religion would be determined by its ruler — a suitably German dictum.

For the next sixty-three years the two camps prepared for the ultimate trial of strength, the spark coming when the childless Emperor Matthias nominated Ferdinand of Styria, a fanatical Catholic, as his successor in Bohemia. Bohemia had a Protestant majority, an elective monarchy and the Habsburgs had long regarded it as a private possession. The Bohemians rose against the Emperor's diktat, throwing his legates from a high window during the famous Defenestration of Prague (1618). Instead of Ferdinand, the Bohemians nominated the leading German Calvinist prince, Frederick, Elector Palatine, as their King. Unfortunately for them, Frederick was a vague, dithering bloke — though he was married to rather a fine Stewart, Elizabeth, the 'Winter Queen', daughter of James VI & I. Ferdinand was elected Emperor in succession to Matthias and the Thirty Years War broke out, involving just about every European government on one side or the other. Fought in the name of religion, this bloody conflict, basically, was a dynastic struggle between the Habsburgs and the Bourbons, with Germany providing the bulk of the cannonfodder and battlefields. (France came in only in 1635.) Between a half and a third of the German population perished, as mercenary armies fought, ravaged and laid waste the land, sacked great cities, burned villages, brought death, starvation, plague, syphilis and cannibalism —

THAT WAS BLOODY SILLY—
CLAIMING CATHOLICS COULD FLY!

a real religious conflict, with the chief brains supplied by a cardinal, Cardinal Richelieu, of France. Throughout, the German princes, regardless of religion, continued to play their endless pigheaded wargames to frustrate the emergence of any real central government. The war and the Peace of Westphalia (1648) finished the Habsburgs as a threat to the French. They also finished the Empire: Austria, Bavaria, Saxony and Brandenburg emerged as sovereign states; Sweden got Pomerania; the Prince of Transylvania overran Moravia.

The only Germans to benefit from this ghastly mayhem were the Hohenzollerns in remote Brandenburg. Here, Frederick, the first Elector had spent his time subduing the native nobility, the Junkers. His sons, Frederick the Iron and Albert Achilles subjugated the towns. They were slow, ruthless and thorough. Another Albert made himself Grand Master of the Teutonic Knights just in time to disband the Order at the Reformation and so become hereditary Duke of Prussia. As elsewhere, the Thirty Years War brought ruin: fields returned to moor and bog, the Berliners – not for the last time – were reduced to eating dogs and rats. But Frederick William, the 'Great Elector', brought in hard-working Dutch and Huguenots to repopulate and rebuild his shattered territories. He helped the Dutch against the French, and drove the Swedes out of Brandenburg at the Battle of Fehrbellin, 1675. His son, Elector Frederick III received the title King (i.e. King Frederick I of Prussia) from the Emperor Leopold in 1701. King Frederick was a foppish little fellow, who ran rapidly through the Great Elector's savings transforming his court into a smaller version of Versailles. His son detested him.

The creator of the world's first modern autocracy, Frederick William I (1713–40) was known in his time, derisively, as the Sergeant King. With a five-foot girth he was not a very likely looking person to establish an autocracy, but then neither was Adolf Hitler. He inherited a bankrupt state and made it the most prosperous in Europe. He made the Junkers his servants, and created an efficient civil service from the middle classes. Most of his subjects remained serfs, and it was one of his strengths that he was in some ways a peasant himself. All the disconnected fragments of his kingdom were subjected to relentless centralist authority. Military men, posing as tax collectors raised vast sums with scrupulous efficiency, most of the proceeds going to support the army. He invented marching in step and the call-up. The one extravagance he allowed himself was his Potsdam Giant Guards, a regiment of 7,000 men all over 6ft, recruited or kidnapped from every part of Europe.

By contrast, young Fritz (Frederick), who displayed an early and unfortunate liking for literature, music and Frenchified ways, was not the apple of his father's eye. Frederick William meant to make a soldier out of him, and did so by brute force, his son bearing some horrifying scars, actual and psychological, from the up-bringing. When he became King, Frederick II 1740–1786, was by far the most civilized person ever to rule over Brandenburg-Prussia. He abolished torture and censorship, proclaimed religious liberty, ended delay and class prejudice in the administration of justice and abolished the Giant Guards. He promoted education, drained marshes, insisted that fruit trees be planted along all roads, encouraged industry, revived the Academy of Sciences, imported silk worms and intellectuals, including Voltaire. But at heart, thanks to his father's influence, he was a soldier.

By audacious aggression, Frederick seized Silesia from Austria thus starting the War of Austrian Succession, then to save his own kingdom from extinction at the hands of the Austrians and their allies (France, Russia, Saxony and Sweden) he launched the Seven Years War (1756–63). It was a pretty close-run gamble, and his survival owed not a little to British victories over France in North America and to a change of ruler in Russia. Ten years later, Frederick joined Prussia and Brandenburg geographically by the First Partition of Poland.

His successors – he had no children – were nincompoops, no match for Napoleon and his armies. The kingdom, thrashed at the battles of Jena and Auerstadt, would have disappeared off the map altogether had not the Tsar pleaded with Napoleon at Tilsit (1807) for its retention in truncated form as a buffer state.

It has often been said that the French Revolution changed Germany more than it changed France. Austria, under Emperor Francis II, sent army after army against Napoleon, but in the end mass armies and Napoleonic tactics were too much for the Habsburgs. Eighteenth-century Germany with its 300 separate territories, most of them midget domains, disintegrated. As Austria lost control of long-held imperial territories, the bigger states grabbed what they could in the prevailing chaos. Naturally, those who sided with Napoleon came off best after Austria's final defeat at Austerlitz (1805): Bavaria, Württemberg and Baden. Napoleon set up a Confederation of the Rhine with these and lesser states. In August 1806, Emperor Francis finally declared the end of the Holy Roman German Empire. From then on the Habsburgs were Emperors of Austria.

In Prussia, a spirit of German nationalism resulted from the traumatic effects of the French Revolution. Baron von Stein and Prince von Hardenberg reformed the truncated state, whilst General Scharnhorst and Count von Gneisenau modernised the army. Patriotic volunteers joined in Napoleon's final defeats but this 'War of Liberation' did not lead to a liberal, united Germany as the hopeful, young volunteers expected. The Congress of Vienna (1815), under the guidance of the reactionary Austrian Prince Metternich, established a federation of thirty-nine princely states and four free cities, with Austria as hereditary president – virtually a tidied-up Holy Roman Empire. A later customs union, the Zollverein, was the only real step towards unity. Territorially, however, Prussia did well out of the Peace: she gained half of Saxony, recovered lost territory east of the Elbe, including large chunks of Poland, as well as much of Westphalia, Swedish Pomerania and, ominously, the Rhineland. A wave of reaction stamped out any manifestation of liberalism or German nationalism.

Reaction triumphed again in 1848, the 'Year of Revolutions', after bourgeois liberal nationalists briefly took over Berlin and waved their black, red and gold flags. Other German governments were completely toppled. Even Metternich resigned. A National German Assembly met at Frankfurt, produced a consti-tution and offered the national crown to King Frederick William IV of Prussia, who politely declined to 'pick up a crown from the gutter'. The movement, like similar ones elsewhere in Europe – in Spain, for example – lacked real mass support. Most of the liberals who weren't shot fled to the United States.

Just as it had needed Napoleon to kick the Germans out of their mini-state medievalism, so it required another masterful leader, Prince Otto von Bismarck, to kick them into national unification, and this he accomplished not for noble liberal motives but purely in the interests of Prussian *realpolitik*.

Nationalism had grown by the 1860s, the result partly of the increase in state-controlled education, partly of the growth of the popular press and partly of the Zollverein, which accustomed Germans to unity and Prussian leadership. Bismarck, a Junker, saw Austria as the obstacle to a complete Prussian take-over of Germany, and as nationalism got a grip on the populations of Central and Eastern Europe, the Habsburg Empire, consisting of diverse nationalities, weakened. The Prussian King, William I, was more pliable in Bismarck's hands than his predecessor, Frederick William IV. Following a short, sharp war against Denmark in 1864, Bismarck defeated a bungling Austrian army at Sadowa in 1866, and the Austrian-dominated German Confederation was replaced by a Prussian one. Europe was surprised: it was the first of many short sharp shocks from a suddenly modern, industrialising Germany. The Prussian commander, Count Helmut von Moltke had foreseen that modern industries held the key to great military might: railways, the telegraph, machine-tooled cannon and breech-loading rifles could flatten the enemy before it got organised. In an attempt to counter the rising tide of nationalism, the Habsburgs, resourceful to the last, now set up an Austro-Hungarian Empire, by devolving power to their largest and most troublesome subjects, the Magyars. Their defeat deeply worried the French, whose position had long depended on manipulating Austro-Prussian rivalry. Napoleon III, with little understanding of the sort of changes von Moltke was effecting, sought to redress the balance. Bismarck obliged, crushing the French Second Empire at Sedan (1870) and proclaiming the reluctant King William Kaiser of the Second Reich – the Holy Roman Empire being the first one – at Versailles the following year. The constitution of the Confederation was expanded to encompass the other German states, and Alsace-Lorraine was annexed from the French.

Bismarck ruled Germany as Imperial Chancellor for the next two decades. Nationalism had now become the most dynamic force in European politics, and it was part of Bismarck's genius that he was able to develop it as an anti-democratic force in the new Germany. Industrialisation was speeded up: by 1893 Germany had overtaken Britain in steel production, and output of electricity was twice that of Britain by 1913. Urban population outstripped rural, and agriculture ceased to be the most important activity. As part of his strategy to deprive emerging socialist parties of mass support, Bismarck introduced health and accident insurance and old-age pensions.

The new Empire remained a feudal, authoritarian state, and Bismarck's domestic policies were all designed to maintain it as such. His foreign policy after 1871 was designed to secure peace, which he did with a web of alliances, notably the League of Three Emperors (Germany, Austria and Russia), and by acting as 'honest broker', as at the Congress of Berlin (1878) between the conflicting interests of Austria and Russia in the increasingly turbulent Balkans.

Success guarantees the continuance of authoritarian systems, and Bismarck's successes were so great and various that his system would have continued even if he had been succeeded by a complete nincompoop. He was. The death of Kaiser William I in 1888 and that of his son Frederick three months later ushered in Kaiser William II, who had certifiable lunatics on both sides of his ancestry. From 1897 he himself was the mainspring of all policy, with a rapid growth of German global ambitions, imperialism and racism. The loony doctrine of the superiority of the 'Aryan' race became fashionable. Admiral Tirpitz and Count von Bülow, together with various loud-mouthed pressure groups demanding Germany's 'place in the sun', were the main influences on William. Tirpitz, Minister of Marine, created a vastly enlarged navy – to the horror of the British. The army, given the quality of the Kaiser's leadership, pursued its own policies under General Count von Schlieffen – father of the famous Plan. Officers drank to 'The Day'. Every able-bodied German male served three years' conscription.

The Kaiser alienated Germany's natural allies, Britain and Russia. Bismarck's treaties were allowed to lapse, his moderating hand on Austria's recurrent Balkan crises was replaced by confusion and sabre-rattling. Britain, France and Russia drew closer together. The Kaiser ranted on about Encirclement. Inevitably, 'The

Day' arrived: 1 August 1914. The idiot had brought death to almost every home from Moscow to Unst.

Crowds danced, sang and marched in Berlin, but they did the same in London, Paris and St Petersburg. The Schlieffen Plan rolled forward, fell apart and the whole point was lost. The armies dug in and slaughtered each other in meaningless offensives in no man's land. The Russian autocracy collapsed. The Royal Navy slowly starved the Germans. Kaiser Bill became a meaningles cipher disregarded completely by his own generals. Bull-necked, General Ludendorff, an ardent believer in total war, became the real leader. Unrestricted German U-boat warfare, a desperate attempt to break the British blockade, brought the fresh-faced confident soldiers of the United States of America into the war against the Fatherland, and when Ludendorff's Final Offensive narrowly failed in spring 1918, he warned the politicians of total social collapse if they did not make an armistice. While US President Wilson refused to deal with the 'militarists', the German navy mutinied, red flags appeared in the towns, and in Berlin Karl Liebknecht prepared for a Soviet Republic. Hindenburg persuaded the Kaiser to flee and the war ended. If he had abdicated sooner, they could have saved the dynasty and spared Germany and the whole of Europe the subsequent horrors of Nazism and another World War.

Thrilling and fateful days followed. The pro-establishment classes – which included a lot more than Prussian Junkers – feared what Ludendorff had predicted: red revolution as was happening in Russia and as the Great Peasants' War had so nearly unleashed in Luther's time. There was also a widespread conviction that Germany had not lost the war militarily but had been betrayed from inside by treacherous elements such as Communists, intellectuals, non-'Aryans' and Jews.

With the breakdown of the Kaiser's government, the Social Democrat leader, Ebert became Chancellor with 30 per cent of the vote – such as it was – in daily danger from Spartacists and other revolutionaries. Soldiers and Workers Soviets were springing up all over the place. People bought cheap guns from returning soldiers. A People's Naval Division occupied part of the Imperial Palace. A Soviet Republic was proclaimed in Bavaria. Spartacists rioted everywhere. The victorious allies failed to agree and the blockade was continued while starving, unemployed soldiers and refugees swarmed into the cities. On 6 January 1919, Liebknecht and his Spartacists, with practically no support launched their putsch and were joined by other red groups, taking over government buildings and barricading Ebert into the chancellery. It seemed that Germany was going exactly the same way as Russia.

A counter-revolution however, had already been sprung. The military High Command pledged support for Noske, the Minister of Defence, various officers having organised their own *Frei Korps* of tough, veteran soldiers who did not want to be demobilised. These units marched on Berlin led by Noske, equipped with machine guns, tanks and armoured cars, and proceeded to smash the Spartacists with brutal efficiency. Liebknecht was shot, as was Rosa Luxemburg – a famous Spartacist female. It was all over in a week, and

Ebert's provisional government was back in control, but backed by Freikorps bayonets.

The Germans had marched willingly into the valley of death on the orders of triflers and pig-headed militarists. The next twenty years took them into a further hell as their economy collapsed, unemployment rocketed, traditional and moral values declined and the rats emerged from the shadows to take over the Reich and give it a brothel glory based on racism, violence, slavery, terror and concentration camps.

The Weimar Republic of the inter-war years failed to gain genuine support, not surprisingly in view of the traumas and problems it had to grapple with and because democracy had never before been tried in Germany. Now that it was, it was at once associated with a lot of things people didn't like: reparations imposed by the Treaty of Versailles, war guilt, economic collapse. With the renewed fear of a 'red threat', the High Command concluded that their best hope of saving Germany from what had happened in Russia lay in Hitler and his National Socialist German Workers' Party. Hindenburg appointed Hitler Chancellor in January, 1933, because his party had more votes than any other.

The new Reichs Chancellor had been around the seedy, violent perimeter of Weimar politics for a long time by 1933. Backed by Ludendorff, he had attempted the Beer Hall Putsch in Munich in 1923, and put his ideas down on paper in *Mein Kampf* during his resulting term behind bars. His party attracted a miscellaneous clientèle of drifters, anti-semites, crackpots and adventurers, just like any other political party. Hitler was their prize asset and he owed much of his appeal to the gutter press.

By the end of 1933, following the passage of an Enabling Act whereby the Reichstag virtually voted for its own death warrant, Hitler was a dictator and Germany completely in his power, the only real opposition lying in the genuine socialist elements in his own party. These were eliminated by the Night of the Long Knives, or Rohm Purge of 1934. For many Germans disillusioned by the post-war settlement and the effects of the depression the Nazis, like the Devil, sang some good tunes: they offered strong leadership, unemployment vanished, business men got contracts, Germany rearmed and brought off spectacular successes in foreign affairs. By 1938, with Austria, the Rhineland and Czechoslovakia in the bag, Hitler could purge sixteen generals from the army with perfect impunity. As for the churches, apart from a very few men such as Niemöller who stood against the regime, the least said the better.

By the time the cynical and feckless politicians in the British and French governments decided Hitler had gone too far, in 1939, it was too late. By then the Nazis had created a formidable military machine, and virtually the whole of Germany was marching, once again, behind it. The Nazi-Soviet Pact of 1939 released Hitler from Bismarck's old fear of war on two fronts. The Red Army advanced to meet them to a pre-arranged line, and Poland (September 1939) and the Baltic states (1940) disappeared off the map. In April, 1940, the Germans overran Norway and Denmark, smashed through Holland, Belgium, Luxemburg, flanked the French Maginot line, forced the British evacuation at Dunkirk, and blitzkrieged France into surrender within five weeks. In Berlin, children strewed rose petals before the Fuhrer's Mercedes. German casualties were fewer than in the Franco-Prussian war. Germany was indeed, as Hitler had promised, master of Europe, and if 1940 had been the end of it, he and his henchmen would be as revered today by his countrymen as Napoleon and his marshals have long been by the French. The Thousand Year Reich was not a ludicrous concept in 1940; the Holy Roman Empire had lasted that long.

By 1945 it was all over. The cities were reduced to rubble, the Russians pillaged their way across the land and the British, Americans and French poured in as conquerors. And with the revelation of the scale of the concentration camp atrocities the Germans were regarded as pariahs. Hitler had fallen for his own myth, spread his forces ever thinner, like Napoleon, and taken ever greater and ever more unrealistic risks. His luck ran out. Only months after the invasion of the USSR, the declaration of war on the USA, December, 1941, was folly. Another factor was that the Nazi state was at no time as totalitarian as Stalin's – nor arguably as Churchill's. Despite popular mythology, the New Order was in fact a prey to bureaucratic and administrative inefficiency and needless triplication, and after the dismissal of Hitler's economic whizzkid Hjalmar Schacht it was downhill all the way. The size of present day bureaucracies makes Hitler look like Ludwig of Bavaria. Far more surprising is that after two World Wars in which the Germans were shown to be people who would follow crazy leaders with invincible determination, the battered victors actively rebuilt the land as a nation – albeit unavoidably in two bits till 1990. More than thirty million people had been killed. The most salutary course would have been to ensure the Germans went back to living as they had done till 1870, in a land of many principalities. The cold war dictated otherwise: both sides, the USSR and the West, set about reviving its own Germany as a bulwark and a showcase.

Poland seized East Prussia, Silesia and parts of Brandenburg and Pomerania. The USSR annexed the north of Prussia. The rest of the country was divided into four zones, with Berlin likewise split in four between Russians, Americans, British and French. Stalin expelled 4 million refugee Germans from Poland, Hungary and Czechoslovakia, worsening the huge problem of 'displaced persons' starving in bomb-sites and old shelters. The cigarette was the only currency: with 200 fags you could buy anything. Not that there was much left to buy.

New *Länder*, federal states, were set up in 1947, eleven in the West; five old *Länder* in the East. Prussia disappeared off the map. By 1948 relations between West and East had deteriorated to the Berlin Airlift stage, and continued to be unfriendly throughout the next forty-two years – the Berlin Wall, Checkpoint Charlie and the suppression of a Workers' Rising in East Germany in 1953 – until the sudden collapse of the Honecker regime, together with the whole Communist house of Stalinist concrete in 1990. West Germany, thanks to the US Marshall Plan, Ludwing Erhard and the rapid revival of the traditional German virtues of hard work, order and enterprise, participated in – indeed led – the revival of Europe after 1945. The Chancellor, Konrad Adenauer, worked hard at making his country respectable again: she became a member of NATO and the European Coal and Steel Community, was reconciled with

I ALWAYS THINK THERE'S SOMETHING TRULY GERMAN ABOUT SOCIALISM, HERMAN.

France, made reparations to Israel. Her millions of homeless, destitute refugees – not to mention hundreds of thousands of *Gast-Arbeiters* – were absorbed into her economic miracle.

By the 1980s, the Federal Republic of West Germany had again become the most powerful nation in Europe. Prosperity appeared to make the vast majority of its citizens apolitical. The peace-loving *Bundeswehr* (Federal Army) advertised in vain for officer material. The division between East and West had become wearily accepted until on 3 October 1990 it disappeared.

For once, history has a clear message for the future: on past showing, a united Germany needs careful watching.

GREECE

And now for something completely different. At opposite ends of the European Community are two states who share little of the common history, for whom Charlemagne, the Rise and Fall of Burgundy and Bourbon-Habsburg rivalry might as well have occurred on Pluto. Of these two, Ireland does not even share a common Roman antiquity, but, whilst Ireland was for long dominated by the English, Greece alone has spent some 400 years since 1400 under the rule and occupation of a non-European, non-Christian empire. And it shows: Greece is still more Balkan and Levantine than West European.

And yet the Ancient Greeks invented Europe. Living by sea-borne trade, piracy and fishing in a barren, mountainous land with innumerable islands, they were a very adventurous, resourceful bunch – or, rather, bunches because they

THE LEGACY OF GREECE : PANDORA'S BOX.

never voluntarily formed one political nation, wisely choosing to restrict the ill effects of politics (which they also invented) to small, manageable units, until coralled into vast empires by Alexander, the Romans and then the Turks.

Their earliest effort at European civilisation was the result of trade between Crete and Ancient Egypt. This produced, *c.* 1500 BC, some very decent vases, bull-leaping and King Minos and the Minotaur. Unfortunately it all slid under the sea one afternoon as a result of great volcanic eruptions at Thira (Santorini) in the Aegean. Such carelessness was hardly the style of the Mycenaeans, who launched a second attempt to found European civilisation, *c.* 1200 BC, with Homeric types – Agamemnon, Helen of Troy, King Priam, Hector, Odysseus – Bronze Age hero sailors, shipbuilders and entrepreneurs with a great taste for the epic exaggeration.

An Iron Age period of invasions and instability followed during which the *polis* developed as a walled place of refuge centred on its acropolis, the fortress on the hill. By the late 6th and 5th centuries, BC, new forms of government were being tried: tyrants, oligarchs, democracy – especially, of course, in Athens. Enterprising colonists traded all over the Mediterranean and beyond. Those in Asia Minor were a source of irritation to Darius and Xerxes, great kings of the Persian empire who tried and failed to destroy Athens, 490–480 BC. It was a near thing for Europe. The Golden Age of Athens ensued, the brief, brilliant period of Classical Greece, the sparkling well from which the mainstreams of European civilisation have flowed ever since.

The Ancient Greeks may have only tenuous links genetically with modern Greeks but they shared key characteristics. They were interminably fractious, and the subtle complexities of their disputes were far more important to them than reaching workable political solutions. They were thus fairly easy prey to civil wars and to determined imperialists such as Alexander and the Romans who, once they had conquered, proceeded to absorb and spread Greek civilization over their empires. Unfortunately for the Romans, however, in their dogged desire to acquire culture, it wasn't the Greeks of pristine Classical Antiquity they were copying but the decidedly unprincipled, slippery, sophisticated rogues and charmers of the Hellenistic or Antiochene period of Greek culture. Greek became the *lingua franca* – if that is the *mot juste* – of the eastern parts of the Roman Empire; Greek teachers, sophists, artists, craftsmen, mountebanks, and religious enthusiasts were highly regarded by all who could afford their services.

For an almost unbelievably long time, this Hellenistic Roman civilisation, conjoined to Greek Christian Orthodoxy, withstood the onslaughts of barbarian invasions on the Eastern Roman Empire, centred on Byzantium, Constantinople, from 395 to 1453. Frequently and ignorantly characterised as fossilised and corrupt, it had a unique capacity for self-renewal in the face of disastrous odds. Byzantium in the Dark Ages was the only surviving civilised city in the whole of Europe. Gradually, by innumerable battles and some appalling treacheries, its

Empire grew smaller and smaller as its provinces were wrested from it one by one, till 1453 when, with a massive fleet and many cannon, the Ottoman Turks finally overthrew it, and the last Greek Emperor, Constantine XI, died fighting on the massive walls. With typical Greek paradox, this last catastrophic period was a time of cultural renaissance.

Greece itself had long since fallen prey to a wide variety of foreign invaders, like any of the other provinces of Byzantium: Normans, Genoese, Angevins, Catalans and Venetians, most of whom had established principalities and duchies, like Shakespeare's Duchy of Athens. These were now, apart from the Venetians in Corfu and a few other islands, shoved out and replaced for all Greeks by the pashas, janissaries and firmans of the Sultan in Istanbul.

The Turks continued on across the Balkans till 1683, when they failed to take Vienna. Thereafter they went into slow territorial retreat in Europe, accompanied by increasing governmental corruption and incompetence. External powers were immediately keen to exploit its growing weakness. Peter the Great (1682–1725) began the Tsarist policy of aiding Greek rebels. Bands of brigands called *klephts* operated from the mountains and from numerous islands as pirates. Irregular troops called *armatoloi* were raised by the Turkish authorities to deal with them, but these soon became merely rival guerrilla bands. Tsar Peter used crudely printed leaflets to foster messianic myths that a fair-haired race from the north would bring deliverance. Various Russo-Turkish wars in the eighteenth century kept such hopes alive.

Following the failure of Sultan Selim III (1789–1807) to reform the Ottoman government, the Empire fell more and more into the hands of local strong men

and, in some places, into the hands of *Phanariots*, a Greek elite who had started as diplomatic interpreters and become indispensible, as Turkish governments had perforce to have more dealings with foreign powers. The *Phanariots* expanded their grip on top jobs in the corrupt Ottoman bureaucracy, becoming governors of islands and, in Moldavia and Wallachia (Romania) hospodars (princes). Here, with their hangers-on and relatives the Phanariots grew rich on rapacity, corruption and intrigue, but their courts were also centres of reviving Greek culture and channels of influence from Western Europe. At the same time, Greek merchants were taking an ever larger share of Ottoman commerce and shipping, several making fortunes by blockade-running during the Napoleonic Wars. There was also a small Western-educated intelligentsia struggling out into the light of nineteenth-century liberalism, keen on reviving the Ancient Greek heritage, but such people were soon diverted by an interminable argument about whether the Ancient Greek language should be revived or whether the ordinary demotic Greek of the day should be retained with all its Slavic, Turkish and Italian accretions, or whether a purefied new demotic national language should be created. This argument has gone on from then till the present day.

So far, thanks to Johnny Turk, the Greeks had been spared the damaging effects of European history. Even the Sublime Porte, however, could not stop the dire effects of the French Revolution and Napoleonic Wars from reaching into this Ottoman backwater. Napoleon invaded Egypt, an Ottoman possession, taking the Ionian Islands *en passant*, and these finished up in 1815 as 'a single, free and independent state under the exclusive protection of His Britannic Majesty', soon becoming a convenient refuge for mainland klephts, some of whom picked up useful military experience by enlisting in the Duke of York's Greek Light Infantry. This was the beginning of the British Empire's increasing role as a protector, which was to last till that Empire also ran out of steam in the late 1940s.

Serbia had revolted from Ottoman rule in 1804 and acquired semi-independent status. Greek secret societies sprang up, one of which managed an invasion of Moldavia and Wallachia, which the Ottomans suppressed in 1821. Simultaneous risings in the Peloponnese sparked off fashionable European concern; funds and motley volunteers began arriving, many of them becoming rapidly disillusioned on finding that the rude and commercially minded klephts and armatoloi bore little resemblance to the fabled heroes of Thermopylae. Pushkin found the Greeks 'a nasty people of bandits and shopkeepers'. Lord Byron however, with greater aplomb, did the Greek cause considerable good by dying (1824) at Missolonghi, thereby attracting a great deal of Romantic attention to the struggle – and to his posthumous reputation. Naturally, the Greeks spent most of their energies on fratricidal arguments about the type of society they were fighting for. Two rival provisional governments were set up, one led by Kolokotronis, a captain of klephts, the other under one George Koundouriotis, described as 'a prominent Hydriot of Albanian descent'. Basically, the division was between the fighting men on the one hand, who wanted a traditional, kilt-wearing society, and on the other the Western educated minority, who

appealed a lot more to progresives in the West, had considerably more political nous, and access to Western loans. This group wanted to introduce a Western-style modern society. The considerable gap between these two groups has continued ever since.

Officially, the European Powers had so far maintained their post-Napoleonic reactionary rigidity: no help to rebellions anywhere. When the Ottomans sent in Mehmet Ali, Pasha of Egypt, to suppress the Greek rebels, however, anguished cries for help echoed around the chancelleries of Europe till, activated by mutual suspicion that the others would act unilaterally, Britain, France and Russia drew up the Treaty of London (1827), which proposed the setting up of an autonomous – though not independent – Greek state. The Turks' response to this piece of interference included massacres and a big push by Mehmet Ali, whereupon a British expedition under General Sir Richard Church and Admiral Lord Cochrane arrived. The two rival provisional governments were forced to amalgamate and a sometime foreign minister of the Tsar's Dominions, Count John Capodistrias, a Corfiot, was invited to become president. The Turks dispatched a fleet, which the British sank at the Battle of Navarino Bay (1827). Count John tried hard to create the basis of a nation where none had ever existed, but most of the influential sections of the population were against him, used as they were to the lax rule of the Turk. He was assassinated in 1831 on his way to church.

The resulting anarchy had to be dealt with by Britain, France and Russia since they had been mainly responsible for creating it. With the insouciance that was possible only in the nineteenth century, they appointed one Prince Frederick Otto von Wittelsbach, a seventeen-year-old son of King Ludwig of Bavaria, as hereditary King of Greece. They also provided 60 million francs for the Prince to be going on with, and a British gunboat to take him there in 1833.

King Otto had problems from the start, as well as a Regency Council of Bavarians and some 3500 Bavarian troops to help him solve them. His kingdom was only about a third the size of the present country, the whole place swarmed with irregular troops and bandits, and Greeks continued to emigrate back into the Ottoman Empire. With Teutonic energy and single-mindedness, the Regency Council worked hard to impose a totally Bavarian governmental apparatus, whilst Otto, a Roman Catholic, was declared head of the Church, then suppressed 412 out of 593 monasteries, forfeiting their property to the Crown.

An uprising in 1844 resulted in a constitution and a parliament, but Otto continued to wield most of the power. He gained some popularity by adopting a 'Greater Greece' policy – to unite all Greeks with the kingdom – but the response was less than enthusiastic from Greeks living outside, because they were in an increasingly strong position in the Ottoman Empire, especially in shipping, banking, commerce, railways and diplomacy.

After King Otto's deposition in 1862, it took the Protecting Powers a year to find any princeling willing to take on the job. Eventually they came up with Prince Christian William Ferdinand Adolphus George of

Holstein-Sonderborg-Glucksburg, who, as King George I of the Hellenes, had many influential relations among European Royalty and the good sense to spend a large part of each year, visiting them. As a goodwill gesture, the British threw in the Ionian Islands, and a new constitution limited the royal powers, though they remained considerable.

Greek politics continued in the pattern they had already developed: a restricted political class spent ephemeral periods in office rewarding their supporters with jobs and any other perks that happened to come their way. Elections were far from clean. Brigandage remained a way of life. There were recurrent crises in the Balkans to profit from if possible, as at the Congress of Berlin (1878) when Greece was given control of Thessaly and part of Epirus from the declining Turkish Empire. The Prime Minister, Trikoupis, laboured long and hard to drag and kick the country into modern times: when he came to power in 1882 there were but seven miles of railway. But his many improvements were undone by his rival Deliyannis on his election. The Powers had again to intervene, as international confidence in Greece slumped. Between 1890 and 1914, about a sixth of the population emigrated to the United States, their remittances becoming a major element in maintaining such financial stability as the country had. In 1897 an International Financial Control Commission had to be set up with representatives from Britain, France, Russia, Germany, Austria-Hungary and Italy to oversee Greece's international debt repayments.

Balkan feuds of bewildering complexity became steadily more hectic as the twentieth century dawned. Greeks and Bulgars worked puppet agitators in Macedonia, Greeks often working hand in glove with their old enemy the Turks against the Bulgars. In 1910, however, Eleftherios Venizelos, a veteran Cretan guerrilla (Crete having gained autonomous status from Turkey in the 1890s) came to power with something like a popular mandate and the support of King George. Liberal reforms won him more support in 1912, and the two Balkan Wars of 1912 and 1913 gave scope for his wily Cretan skills as a negotiator: by the resulting Treaty of Bucharest (1913) Greece increased its areas by 70 per cent and its population from 2.8 to 4.8 million by the acquisition of most of Macedonia and the whole of Crete. Despite the assassination of King George in 1913, Venizelos's triumph created unusual national unity.

It did not last. The First World War split the country, with King Constantine I – trained at a Prussian military academy and married to the Kaiser's sister – favouring strict neutrality and Venizelos looking to his good relations with Lloyd George to secure further national benefits in return for Greek help against Austria-Hungary. Lloyd George, however, besides being as great a rogue as Venizelos, had other fish on his line. When Turkey entered the War on the German side, the main British priority in the Balkans was to prevent Bulgaria going the same way, so parts of Macedonia that Greece had just secured were now promised to the Bulgars by the Welsh Wizard. Venizelos was persuaded to go along with this only in return for British promises of 'territorial concessions on the coast of Asia Minor'. Lloyd George omitted to tell his Greek chum he had promised exactly the same concessions to the Italians.

Further divisions between King and Prime Minister arose over Venizelos's wish to participate in the Dardanelles campaign. John Metaxas, Acting Chief of Staff, resigned, believing the whole campaign was ill advised and that the Greek army would be incapable of holding on to any concessions in Asia Minor: in both cases, Metaxes was later proven right. Venizelos resigned, the country slid towards civil war, but an election returned Venizelos again.

Bulgaria had meanwhile joined Germany, and Serbia was in big trouble as a result. Venizelos wished to allow British and French troops access through Greece to help the Serbs, but King Constantine refused, whereupon Venizelos once again resigned. The British and French landed at Salonika – where a pro-Venizelos rival government was established – and seized Corfu. By 1916 they had also seized Athens, recognised the Salonika government and forced Constantine into exile, his second son Alexander succeeding him on the throne. Venizelos in true Greek style proceeded to purge State and Church of his opponents. Nine Greek divisions were sent to the Macedonian Front, where they proved a decisive factor in determining the Germans to sue for peace; a further two divisions were dispatched to Russia with the grand aim of trying to 'strangle Bolshevism at birth'.

Naturally, he was determined to reap his reward when the fighting stopped. By the Treaty of Sèvres (1920), despite Italian efforts and the activities of Turkish irregulars, Greece was granted a five-year protectorate over Smyrna and district – on the coast of Asia Minor – to be followed by a plebiscite on whether the area should become part of Greece. They were also granted the Dodecanese and Aegean Islands and most of Thrace. It looked like a triumph for Venizelos; in fact, nemesis was upon the threshold. In Turkey the decayed Ottoman Sultanate had been replaced by Kemal Atatürk, the man who single-handedly was to create and modernise a Turkish nation. He swore to lose no inch of Anatolia. In Greece, King Alexander died of a monkey bite and his two brothers refused to succeed him. Venizelos unexpectedly lost the post-war election, and the exiled King Constantine returned to the throne, opposed by Britain and France, who were now supporting Atatürk as a bulwark against Bolshevism. Constantine invaded Turkey in March 1921, his army reaching within forty miles of Ankara, whereafter it was pushed back and routed by Atatürk. The Turks never did things by halves and proceeded to massacre the whole Christian population of Smyrna – about 30,000 people – dramatically ending the Greek presence in Asia Minor that had predated Darius the Great. About a million Turkish-speaking refugees descended upon Greece, others taking their entrepreneurial skills all over the Middle East and down into Africa, where their descendants remain to this day, G*d bless them. The triumph had turned into a national disaster.

A revolutionary committee seized power and King Constantine abdicated, to be succeeded by his eldest son George II. War – criminal politicians were executed. By the Treaty of Lausanne (1923), Greece lost most of its paper gains, and various populations were exchanged between Greece and Turkey. To cope with the immense influx of refugees, big landed estates were broken up to provide small farms, and there were international loans. This ensured the complete fragmentation – and inefficiency – of Greek agriculture but at least provided for a large landowning peasantry, a sound bulwark against Communism. Urban refugees were worse off, congregating in shanty towns around Athens and Salonika. It was the refugees who swung a plebiscite in 1924 in favour of abolishing the monarchy, and the Communist party now began to increase its support in urban areas.

A number of ineffective republican governments followed, and a military dictatorship under General Pangalos, 1925–26, which launched a brief invasion of Bulgaria and issued a decree forbidding women to raise their skirts. The General was overthrown by a *putsch*, the most fashionable form of governmental change in those days. Venizelos made a comeback between 1928 and 1932, bringing some welcome stability and a pragmatic policy of mending fences with neighbours – Italy, Yugoslavia, Albania Bulgaria, and even, in 1930, with Turkey.

Putsches and purges were the order of the day thereafter. Venizelos was forced into exile, sentenced to death *in absentia*, and died in 1936. A rigged plebiscite restored the monarchy, Communist electoral support grew and labour unrest mounted as a result of the Depression and general strikes. In such circumstances, the only course open was the one King George chose in 1936: he brought in a Fascist Dictator.

General John Metaxas set about creating a Third Hellenic Civilisation – the first being Classical Greece, the second Byzantium – which was a tall order given the basic material he was working with. He had himself proclaimed not just 'Leader' and 'National Father' – scarcely original in 1936 – but also 'First Peasant'. He did the sort of things Fascist dictators have to do – close down the parliament, suspend the constitution, denounce liberalism, Communism and parliamentary government in general – and retained the support of the King, the army and a compulsory Youth Organisation. He was also responsible for building roads, introducing an eight-hour day, and starting a national health insurance scheme. He had, as any dictator must have, a highly effective Minister of Public Order, Colonel Maniadakis, who ferreted out plots and underground Communist cells, but alone among dictators he used exile to remote islands – a traditional Byzantine practice – instead of liquidation, and modelled his regime on the successful tyrants of the sixth century BC.

Despite increasing German economic penetration in the 1930s, Metaxas attempted to maintain British friendship, though his proposed alliance was rejected by the feckless British government in 1938. When war broke out, Mussolini, relying on out-of-date intelligence reports, invaded Greece from conquered Albania. In fact, Metaxas had re-equipped his forces and the Italians met with fierce resistance and something of a national uprising – Metaxas's defiance and Greek victory over the Italians is celebrated to this day. Metaxas died in January 1941, and with Hitler tightening his grip on the Balkans in preparation for his invasion of the USSR, Greek attitudes began to waver. Confusion and a bungled, though sizeable, British expeditionary force

led to Hitler's invasion; an unauthorised armistice by General Tsolakoglou, commander of the West Macedonian army (April 1941); the evacuation of the British; and Tsolakoglou being set up as puppet Prime Minister. A gallant British-Greek attempt to hold Crete was flattened by a massive German air attack and paratroop landings. By June, the whole of Greece was under German, Italian and Bulgarian occupation.

The Greeks have always been better at resistance than constructive political action, and their experience of foreign domination went back a long way. Over 350,000 Greeks died in this resistance, in Axis reprisals, executions, concentration camps, fighting or starvation. The Communists played a major part in it, but kept up a popular-front image to avoid alienating conservatives. British secret agents were everywhere, liaising with guerrillas to carry out such exploits as the blowing up of the Gorgopotamus rail viaduct, which held up German supplies to Rommel for weeks on end. Quarrelling was non-stop, and various conferences held around the Mediterranean resulted only in political deadlock. In their mountain enclaves, the Communists demonstrated their ideas for the future to effect: education, health, justice, theatre and women's emancipation. As the Germans withdrew in disorder in 1944, the Communists could easily have taken over the country, the old politicians being universally despised as a failed and corrupt clique. However, an agreement between Churchill and Stalin allowing the latter a free hand in Romania had the curious result of making the Communists fall into line behind a British-inspired exile government led by George Papandreou – who had no popular support, and who returned in October 1944.

Greece was in complete shambles, with rampant inflation. Guerrilla bands ran their own areas. Government by increasingly right wing, inept politicians alternated with direct control by British troops, a Royal restoration and disputed elections. With the ending of hostilities in Europe and the defeat of Churchill in the 1945 general election, the Labour government in London bowed out and persuaded Truman and the United States to take over their role as Protector. With Communist regimes safely installed all over the Balkans, Stalin blew the whistle for the start of the Greek civil war which raged from 1946 till 1949, adding yet more destruction, hatred, atrocities and refugees till Tito in Yugoslavia split with which Stalin and removed the Greek Communists' main support. Massive US aid which strengthened the hard-pressed Greek army also helped a lot.

Thereafter, Greece in the fifties was under virtual US tutelage, and had to be to exist at all. The Cyprus crisis came and went as Britain lost its place in the Mediterranean and the US engineered compromise in the interests of preserving NATO, of which both Greece and Turkey were now members. Economic growth and financial stability sparked a consumer boom among the 25 per cent of the population that had now come to live in Athens. Tourism was built up. Associate EEC membership was secured by Karamanlis, who had replaced General Papagos as Prime Minister in 1955.

He was succeeded by George Papandreou, a leftist, whose spendthrift Socialist policies, chumminess with Balkan regimes and interference with

the army led directly to inflation and right-wing paranoia. A second Cyprus crisis, with Turkish troops poised to invade the island, together with an alleged left-wing army plot involving the Prime Minister's son Andreas, led directly to a putsch by junior army officers, who adapted a NATO contingency plan to come to power April, 1967. It was brilliantly executed, but unfortunately putsches were hardly as acceptable in the Swingin' Sixties as they had been in the Thirties. Martial law was declared, political parties abolished, left wingers rounded up and sent to bleak islands, and beatniks, hippies and mini-skirts were outlawed. The key role of the US in the coup was justified by results: the new government were scrupulously pro-NATO at a time when the build-up of Soviet naval power in the Mediterranean and Arab-Israeli wars (1967 and 1973) made Greek bases of prime importance. The only loser was King Constantine, who bungled a royalist counter-coup, flew out to Rome, and was later deposed.

There was very little popular opposition, outwith the student campuses. When thirty-four students came to sticky end in a protest in Athens, Prime Minister Papadopoulos (also Minister of Defence, Foreign Minister, Minister of Education, Minister of Government Policy and Regent) was deposed amid outraged howls from Europe's liberals. A civilian government took over, but power was held by Brigadier Ionidis, Head of Military Police, who though efficient lacked subtlety and luck. Inflation spiralled with the international oil crisis of 1973–4, and the Turks invaded Cyprus. The junta collapsed almost as suddenly as it had emerged, and Karamanlis was summoned from exile to clean up.

An election and a referendum on the monarchy were held. A new Socialist party, PASOK, was formed by Andreas Papandreou, demanding punishment for all collaborators with the junta, opposition to the monarchy and big deals for the people. Karamanlis with his right-wing New Democracy party won, though the electors gave monarchy the thumbs down. It was back to the old political round and the old political class. Four attempted army putsches came and went in the first six months, while Karamanlis lived on his yacht for safety. Trials of junta-supporters continued. Relations with Turkey and the US were poor. The 1980s brought PASOK to power and Papandreou the younger, a leftist demagogue strong on promises but weak on delivery. Despite the Socialist rhetoric, Greece remains a member of both NATO and the European Community (full membership since '81).

Happy is the land, they say, that has no history. There are European countries that appear to have given up having a history except for responding to external events, but Greece, like Germany, is unlikely to become one of them.

IRELAND

Ireland was neither conquered by the Romans nor overrun by Germanic tribes in the Dark Ages; alone in Western Europe it has remained Celtic. Not for nothing were the tribal genealogists and poets sacrosanct figures in Celtic society: they transmitted legends, a living, consuming force more powerful than chiefs, kings and warriors.

The virtues and faults of the Celts have gone on surfacing in Ireland over and over again to the present day: generosity, hospitality, humour, heroism, a love of music and celebration, poetry and carousing, tribalism, incapacity to unite against a common foe, fecklessness, a delight in mischief and fighting for its own sake, an inability to compromise effectively and to adapt to change.

As in the Western Highlands of Scotland, this was a self-perpetuating system: the feuds went on for ever and ever, and so did the legends. With no 400-year Roman occupation, no overwhelming barbarian incursions, if Irish Celtic society had been going to develop into something else it could surely have done so: the land is rich and well watered, its advantages many compared, for example, to Holland. But it didn't. The High Kings never established effective control. Raiding and quarrelling were all. With the end of the Roman Empire, they could go on even more epic raids, to Gaul as well as to England, and it was from one such expedition that they brought back the youth Patrick to seven years' swine herding. After his escape and subsequent studies, he returned in AD 432 to Christianise the land of his captivity.

Modern historians assert that there were two Saints Patrick. He was certainly ubiquitous. Before the end of the sixth century, Ireland had become, paradoxically, an important international centre of Latin learning. From its many scattered monasteries great missionaries and teachers, such as Columba and Columbanus, went to Switzerland and Italy as well as to Iona and northern England. There were famous Irish scholars at Charlemagne's court. In Ireland the monks wrote down the language, its legends and records, so that Ireland was the first nation north of Italy to produce a native literature, in books of great beauty. This Golden Age was terminated, around the end of the eighth century, by the coming of the Vikings.

Two centuries of struggle ensued, establishing an unfortunate pattern for later centuries: the Irish would not unite to drive out their invaders, and the invaders were not in sufficient number to dominate and subdue the tribes. The Vikings introduced towns: Dublin, Cork, Waterford, Wexford. At the Battle of Clontarf

BASICALLY WHAT HE'S
SAYING IS: IF YOU WANT TO
STAY OUT OF TROUBLE
EAT GREENS.

(1014), near Dublin, High King Brian Boru – later regarded as a national hero – is supposed to have defeated and restricted the Norsemen. In fact, it was a battle between two Irish factions, one with Norse support, and there are still those, therefore, who denounce King Brian as a usurper.

Legend and fiction have also multiplied around the Norman invasion of 1170, in the reign of the mighty English King Henry II. The Normans were prone to invade wherever they thought they had a sporting chance, but this one had the sanction of Mother Church. The Irish Church, like its daughter set up in Scotland by St Columba, had developed as one of autonomous monastic communities, a pre-feudal Church without hierarchical structure, abbots being more important than bishops. The twelfth-century papacy, asserting supranational control throughout Europe, thoroughly disapproved of it. The Normans were also invited to Ireland, by one Dermot MacMurrough, sometime King of Leinster, who made Richard Strongbow, Earl of Pembroke, an offer he could not refuse: the hand of his daughter in marriage and succession to the Kingdom of Leinster if he could regain it for Dermot. Henry II was involved only because he gave Dermot permission to recruit support among his barons. It might also be borne in mind that Norman barons were not English. There were Normans everywhere, from Scotland to the Holy Land, carving out fiefs for themselves regardless, profiting from their superior military talent and the disunity of the natives.

The trouble, from a dispassionate, non-Celtic viewpoint, was that once again the invaders weren't there in sufficient numbers. The bits they conquered were

AND SEE HERE:
WHAT'S THIS 200 SILVER
GROATS FOR A BLARNEY STONE?

scattered about the country piece-meal, not as one consolidated territory. Celtic society continued to exist as before in pockets within the Norman area, the Pale, and beyond, never achieving a unity that would have allowed them to drive the Normans out.

Medieval English rule in Ireland was spasmodic at best; the great kings were too busy elsewhere. No English king before Henry VIII styled himself King of Ireland. From time to time, efforts were made to regularise the position: in 1366, the Statutes of Kilkenny forbade the Anglo-Normans or English intermarrying with the natives, speaking Gaelic or adopting Celtic customs. The Statutes were not widely observed. Richard II found three classes in Ireland when he visited: 'wild' Irish (Celts), English rebels (Anglo-Normans gone native), and 'obedient' English (English officials). Irish chiefs flocked to meet him to have their authority confirmed by royal decree in return for homage. It was an occasion, something for the tribal bard to strum about in the subsequent long dark winters, but royal authority lasted only as long as the King and his army were physically present. During the Wars of the Roses in the mid-fifteenth century, powerful Norman-Irish families, such as the Butlers and the Geraldines, extended their power at the expense of the Crown, and an Irish parliament asserted its independence from the English one. There was nothing particularly Irish in their actions: barons usually did exploit the weakness of the Crown. Edward IV demonstrated the Crown's continuing ability to strike back at overmighty subjects by executing Thomas, Earl of Desmond, for breaking the Statutes of Kilkenny, but the plain fact of the matter is that Ireland had Home

Rule throughout the Middle Ages, and if it didn't get its act together throughout this long period during which both Celtic and Norman cultures flourished freely it was certainly not the fault of English misrule and exploitation.

The Tudors, however, were an entirely different proposition. The day of the middle-class entrepreneur, new-rich upstart and enterprising small landowner had arrived in England. Worse than that, the Age of the Bureaucrat was dawning. Where you have bureaucrats you have permanent institutionalised meddling, which neither Irish Celts nor modern Highlanders appreciate.

Henry VII, once he had made himself secure on a shaky throne, despatched a typical Tudor new man, Sir Thomas Poynings, to Ireland in 1494, together with an efficient little army and some bureaucrats. They clipped the wings of the ruling Norman-Irish magnate, the Earl of Kildare, and imposed Poynings' Law: that no Irish parliament could initiate legislation without first obtaining the consent thereto of King and Council in England. Then, because he couldn't afford to keep an army permanently in Ireland, Henry released Kildare from the Tower of London to be his deputy there, on the King's own terms – a typical fix by a king renowned for his craftiness.

His son, Henry VIII, was a more meddlesome meddler. He abandoned his father's cost-effective policy, appointed only Englishmen as lieutenants, caused rebellions, sent over an army under Sir William Skeffington. Henry's biggest essay in meddling was, of course, the English Reformation, but it was his Catholic daughter, Queen Mary Tudor, who began the *plantation* of new, armed, English settlers in rebellious areas. Both Celtic Irish and Norman Irish barons were outraged by this: instead of curing rebellion, it provided cause for more serious efforts.

Elizabeth – another product of Henry VIII's meddling – had problems in England with her credibility among Catholics. As far as Ireland was concerned, it could be argued that Henry II had been granted overlordship by a Pope, and now that the English monarchy was no longer Catholic, English rule in Ireland was no longer legitimate. But then, neither was Elizabeth. There were risings, Spanish expeditions, but as ever, they were hopelessly unco-ordinated. More armed settlers were sent in to seize the rebel areas – areas outside the old Pale – and a policy of official terror was employed: executions, wiping out of monasteries, liquidation of bards and teachers, burning of records and looting treasures – Draconian measures by a regime that went in daily fear of being swept away by its own Catholic subjects and the Spanish. Sir Walter Raleigh was one of many dab hands at this butchery. By the time of the Armada, 1588, Elizabeth had her grip on the Irish situation. Shipwrecked Spanish seamen were slaughtered by royal command, not by brutish natives as is somehow often implied. It was only in Ulster that these unfortunates were treated well, for there the Queen's power remained negligible, and it was there that those who opposed the English terror determined to make a stand under a gifted leader, Hugh O'Neill, the nearest the Irish ever got to a national leader, to an Irish Arminius. He built up support slowly for a number of years, helped by Elizabeth's parsimony. Then, at the Battle of Yellow Ford, 1597, he inflicted the severest defeat an English army

ever suffered in Ireland. Risings all over the country followed. The Munster settlers were swept away. The Spanish promised help. Essex, Elizabeth's old favourite, arrived to retrieve the situation and failed, but his successor Mountjoy, a new man in Poynings' mould, wore the Irish down piecemeal, exploited their innate disunity and finally routed them and a small Spanish force at the Battle of Kinsale, 1601.

O'Neill's defeat and the subsequent 'Flight of the Earls', 1607, whereby O'Neill and other Ulster chiefs chose to leave Ireland for the Continent – despite a magnanimous offer by James VI & I to restore their estates to them – were as decisive for Ireland as the Battle of Hastings had been for England. The English set about anglicising the whole country. All the old liberties and Gaelic laws were abolished. English justice and administration was to be extended to every part of the island. Plantations – mainly by King James's native subjects – went ahead on the estates confiscated after the Flight of the Earls, so that Ulster, which had been the last bastion of Celtic resistance, became Loyal.

In Ireland, from Elizabeth's time on, we have the English at their worst: domineering, insufferable, callous, pig-headed, exploitative, incapable of understanding anyone else's language or native culture, racist and dishonest. That the Irish were not without faults we have alluded to already. The two sets of faults put side by side for 300 years bred a bastard and unlovely progeny that combined the worst of both parents, redeemed only on the English side by some superb buildings and on the Irish by the surviving spirit of freedom and the way the people and their church stuck together.

It should be stressed that the anti-Catholic Penal Laws, from which Catholics suffered in Ireland during the seventeenth and eighteenth centuries, were not specifically Irish enactments. They were applied to all Catholics in England by the English Parliament, the result of the Gunpowder Plot of 1605 and of the prevailing anti-Catholic and anti-Spanish feelings that had run high in England since the reign of Mary Tudor. They were designed to ensure that, whilst Catholics would continue to exist in England, they would never attain positions of power; it was illegal for them to own large properties, decent horses, coaches, be well educated, or have any sort of government job, become MPs or vote.

In Stuart times, due to the instability and peculiarities of Stuart sovereigns, these Penal Laws were not rigorously applied in Ireland. The Stuarts tended to look to Ireland as a convenient bolt hole they might need to flee to in emergencies, and they deliberately mitigated the harshness of these laws, with beneficial economic effects. Charles I's Lieutenant General in Ireland, Sir Thomas Wentworth, Earl of Strafford ('Put not your trust in Princes') governed Ireland efficiently, raising and training an Irish army – for which the English Parliament later executed him. But Charles's Anglican Church policy irked Catholic and Ulster Presbyterian alike, and when in 1639 the Scots rose in rebellion against its enforcement in Scotland, the Irish decided to do likewise. They were, as usual, hopelessly divided – the Catholic Celtic Irish, the mostly Catholic Norman Irish, the Protestant English Irish (largely pro-Parliament) and the Ulster Presbyterian Scots Irish.

The rising of 1641 began as a Catholic rebellion in Ulster, and thereafter confusion and backbiting reigned as political and countless other issues became involved. The Earl of Ormonde led a royalist coalition called the Confederacy of Kilkenny (1647), but failed to make the vacillating King Charles come through with definite promises till too late. The papal legate split the Celts from Ormonde, which left the way clear for Cromwell to massacre the whole populations of Drogheda and Wexford. A thorough and callous dispossession of the Irish followed immediately, the majority of Irish proprietors, including most of the old aristocracy, being despatched 'to Hell or Connaught' and replaced by Cromwell's old soldiers and other English. The tables were turned briefly, during the reign of the Catholic James II (1685–9), but when that King was expelled from England by his Parliament for his Catholic policy, he proved an indifferent leader on fleeing to Ireland, although he had widespread Catholic support there. The Ulster settlers made their epic stand, the Apprentice Boys shutting Derry's gates against him and holding out till William of Orange, the new Dutch King of England, arrived to relieve them. Thereafter, James and his Irish army were defeated at the decisive Battle of the Boyne (1690) and James fled to France. Despite William's intention of leniency, Parliament in England was determined to secure English Protestant ascendancy in Ireland once and for all. The remaining rebels capitulated – Patrick Sarsfield being their chief – and fled abroad. This 'Flight of the Wild Geese' removed almost the whole remaining Irish and Norman Irish Catholic aristocracy to the Continent, where they became mercenaries and Jacobites. It also left the mass of the population leaderless.

The new factors in the eighteenth century were: (1) the introduction of the potato in the previous century meant that fewer starved and the population rose above antique levels; (2) the introduction for the first time of English Law and Order meant that people weren't being killed off in tribal wars and English invasions, so population rose above antique levels; and (3) rising rural population created an insatiable demand for little plots of land to grow spuds on, so that English landlords or their agents could rack-rent with impunity.

Having done all in their power to make Ireland a safe place for Protestant settlers, the government's sole concern thereafter lay in ensuring it remained firmly dependent on England politically and commercially – just as with any other eighteenth century colony. The official mercantilist policy of the age was that a colony was supposed to supply England with things the English didn't produce enough of themselves – sugar, tobacco or, in Ireland's case, linen – but they were not allowed to do anything that would bring them into serious commercial competition with English producers. Political restrictions included a tiny electorate easily managed by government fixers, elections called very infrequently, Poynings' Law, and the staffing of all government posts with English or other reliable yes-men.

As in other colonies, the settlers soon found the Mother Country's restrictions cramped their style. Early in the eighteenth century there was an outcry against Wood's halfpence – funny money foisted on Ireland, from which 50 per cent of the profits were to go to one of George I's mistresses – which shows the

SEVENTY ROOMS, AND NOT
A SINGLE ONE WITH A PIG
IN IT, POOR SOULS.

growth of a Protestant Ascendancy 'patriotism' at a time when there was no native Irish political opposition at all. Roman Catholic priests were allowed to function in poverty, while the gross and corrupt Anglican Church of Ireland, financed by tithe payable by the whole population, had virtually no religious significance whatsoever, its churches empty, neglected and ruinous, its bishops either absentee or occupying their blackguard talents as graft-hungry politicians. In Ulster, discriminatory legislation kept Presbyterians out of government posts, and disabled their clergy even from performing marriages – which, paradoxically, Catholic priests could do. But the Ulstermen as tenants had rights, called the Ulster Custom, which Catholics didn't: if they were evicted they had to be compensated for any improvements they had effected to the property – a vital distinction, making for security of tenure and energetic land use. It put them ahead of the game, because it wasn't till the late nineteenth century that such rights were accorded to the Catholic peasantry (and contemporaneously to the disadvantaged crofters of Scotland). They were ahead in other ways as well. As early as 1720 they were preparing to fight the English with their 'Peep o' Day Boys' and later the Orange Order. Emigration from Ulster to the American colonies was high – Ulstermen formed a sixth of the US population by the time of the War of Independence – where they provided some very effective anti-English fighting men.

The loss of the American colonies shook the British government out of its complacency towards its Irish colonists. Fearful of French involvement and the potential of the Irish Volunteer movement (settlers training as Home Guard), they granted a fair measure of free trade and some constitutional reform which didn't amount to much, though it succeeded in splitting the opposition. Entrepreneurs and manufacturers profited from the economic liberalisation. Wealthy families spent more of their year in Ireland, with consequent local economic benefit to shopkeepers and artisans. Dublin became a vigorous capital, with fine buildings, streets and squares.

That part of the opposition which remained unbribed or unconvinced looked to events in France after 1789 with heady enthusiasm. In 1791 Wolfe Tone founded the Society of United Irishmen – which contained practically no Irish Irishmen, composed as it was of 'Patriot' settlers – which the government suppressed as it grew more radical. Irish or not, like every other movement in Ireland it split, and Tone, becoming more republican and separatist, fled abroad to seek help, returning in 1796 with a French force which was only driven off by storms. The government was scared witless and resorted at once to traditional Elizabethan methods: the militia roamed the countryside murdering, burning and torturing as and where informers dictated. The Society's leaders were hanged. Ineffective risings in the south-west and in Ulster came to nothing. The French eventually arrived too late. Tone committed suicide and it was all over.

Convinced in its fear of Irish Jacobins that their previous reforms had gone too far and encouraged all this revolutionary activity, the government forthwith abolished the Irish Parliament in 1800, which it accomplished by creating over a score of peerages and dishing out largesse to disadvantaged owners of pocket boroughs. However, this smart foot-work tripped up over

EQUALITY IS IT?
AND WHO'D BE WANTING
EQUALITY WITH US?

the question of Catholic Emancipation. The worst of the anti-Catholic Penal Laws had been abolished nationwide in 1772, and in 1793 to keep Catholics out of the revolutionary activity Pitt, the Prime Minister, had enfranchised 40-shilling freeholder Catholics in Ireland, i.e. the richer ones. To compensate these enfranchised Catholics for their loss of voting rights when the Irish Parliament was closed down – Catholics in England still had no franchise – Pitt had promised them Catholic Emancipation throughout the UK. However, King George III refused, declaring it was against his coronation oath. Slowly, the disappointment caused by Pitt's broken promise developed into the first ever mass Irish movement, the movement for Catholic Emancipation, led by Daniel O'Connell and funded by penny-a-week contributions. It grew till it could no longer be denied, and Emancipation was granted in 1829 by the Duke of Wellington's Tory government. O'Connell was returned to Parliament, in London, where he chose to work for Ireland for the rest of his career, though many of his followers became sceptical of the efficacy of this tactic as Irish Westminster MPs soon got involved in the endless puppet show there. An attempt in the 1840s to force Peel's government to repeal the Parliamentary Union by similar mass movement came unstuck when Peel called out the dreaded militia. O'Connell hated bloodshed.

The standard of living of the Celtic Irish, had been falling since 1700, as a consequence of rising population. As the government prevented any industries developing that might threaten English ones, peasants had no way to make cash, and came to market infrequently only to barter. With no markets, there was little incentive for landowners to develop their estates, so they were generally absentees, their estates run, or mis-run, by land agents who hiked rents and pocketed the increase. With no resident upper class and no developing local bourgeoisie it was a lot like Communist Eastern Europe in a twisted kind of way: no initiative, no hope and what energy there was diverted into petty racketeering. Famine was often at the door, and the only redress the Irish had against rackrenting and eviction was desperate secret societies like the Whiteboys, who took to terrorising new tenants who came in after evictions.

The economic boom, for settlers, that had occurred during the liberalisation at the end of the eighteenth century did not outlast the Union in 1800. Cheap industrial goods flooded the Irish market, what industries there were collapsed, wages fell, the rich left. The end of the Napoleonic Wars in 1815 ended a long period of agricultural prosperity. Population had increased from 3 million in 1750 to 6 million in 1815, and to 8 million by 1840. The demand for peasant potato plots was insatiable. Government commissions and travellers made frequent reports of the terrible poverty. In Ulster, the 'Ulster Custom', the continuing prosperity of the linen trade and the growth of shipbuilding in Belfast ensured better conditions and a continuing belief in maintaining the link with England. Elsewhere, as reported by a commission on County Mayo: '95 per cent of the population lived in mud huts, food was potatoes and stirrabout, milk was scarce, butter unknown.'

The potato blight of 1845 and 1847 brought famine with terrible suddenness.

Laissez faire (free market economics) – the accepted credo of the day – meant the government would do nothing to interfere with the workings of a free market economy. *The Economist*, that much respected English journal, thought the purge salutary. As a result Ireland continued to export grain, flour, butter, eggs and meat to England while a million Irish starved. Public outcry and private charity caused them eventually to sanction public works, then to open soup kitchens at which 3 million people a day came to be fed. Tenants of more than a quarter of an acre of land were refused soup, so that the starving had to choose between soup and their land. Landlords took the opportunity to get rid of their excess and unwanted tenants: half a million emigrated to the United States in 1847 alone, a quarter-million to Britain. By 1850, population had dropped from 8 to 5 million, to 4 million by 1871, and to 3 million by 1914.

Administration and politics, social and economic commerce went on much the same as usual thereafter, but the Famine was the turning point for English Rule in Ireland. *Laissez faire* or not, no English government would ever have allowed such things to happen in an English county. While most of the effort for Irish Home Rule in the latter half of the century appeared to be made through the parliamentary process – there were 103 Irish MPs at Westminster, often holding the balance between Liberals and Tories, and under Parnell adopting obstructionist tactics that made parliamentary business all but unworkable – it was the direct revolutionary action movement that gained from the Famine. The deaths of a million Irish men, women and children and the continuing forced emigration of a million more were reasons enough to seek freedom through the gun barrel and the bomb rather than the ballot box.

To begin with, the failure of an ineffective rising in 1848 discouraged further efforts. The Famine had bankrupted many landlords and their land went mainly to gombeen men, petty shopkeepers and money-lenders who'd saved a little capital and now used it to set up as fake squireens; potential English and Scottish buyers of bankrupted estates had been put off by the horrors. James Fintan Lalor's message that the land belonged to the people, and that all landlordism was a crime, did not fall on deaf ears. Only in Ulster did industry thrive.

Fenianism was a true revolutionary movement that grew out of the Young Ireland movement of the 1840s forced into exile in the slums of the United States. At its core was the Irish Republican Brotherhood, a secret organisation led by urban intellectuals and activists. Like all Irish movements it had serious splits and no want of police informers. Their first attempt at a rising, in 1867, was no more effective than previous ones, but the Fenians took the action into England itself, where they blew out a wall in Clerkenwell prison and shot a policeman. The culprits were hanged and became the 'Manchester Martyrs'. At the same time, Michael Davitt, a Lalorist, set up the Irish Land League, a legal organisation, to campaign for the 'Three Fs': Fair Rents, Fixity of Tenure, Free Sale. Parnell, leader of the parliamentary Irish allied himself with the League. Bad harvests in 1877–8, more landlord oppression and an agricultural slump in 1880 led to organised boycotts, 'moonlighters' roaming the country, murders, ambushes, maimings and arson. The costs of policing the countryside and keeping landlords safe rocketed. Gladstone granted the Three Fs in 1881; at a stroke, landlords became no more than receivers of rents they couldn't raise. The Conservative government of 1885 passed the Ashbourne Act, which offered peasants state loans to buy their plots outright at 4 per cent interest.

Such radical government action rapidly improved conditions. Sir Horace Plunkett founded an Irish Agricultural Co-operative Society, 1894, to wean Irish peasant farmers away from antique methods and ideas, and get them to set up and join co-operatives. Just about everyone attacked him, but by 1914 there were over a thousand co-ops, mainly creameries. The Nationalists were especially against Plunkett, because as farmers became moderately prosperous they became less inclined to support nationalism. His policies were part of the Conservatives' strategy of 'killing Home Rule by kindness', which, had it been followed consistently would probably have done just that. After all, there's nothing more revolutionary than kindness.

Gladstone and the Liberals had been contemplating Home Rule since the 1880s. It had split their party – the Liberal Unionists eventually joining the Conservatives – done for Parnell (who died in 1891 after a messy divorce scandal) and alternated with Coercion Acts and repression, sparked off by Fenian outrages such as the Phoenix Park murders of 1882. The Liberals were meddlers, like the Tudors, and destined therefore to cause disasters. They were dependent in the Commons on the support of the Irish MPs. When they regained

power from the Tories in 1906, they reopened the Home Rule issue and by 1913 had so succeeded in alienating and inflaming the loyal Protestants of Ulster that there was an army mutiny there – officers refused to countenance using the army to enforce Home Rule on Ulster. A Protestant Volunteer organisation had sprung up which was busy importing guns from Germany, and anti-Catholic feeling was being drummed up by slogans such as *Home Rule is Rome Rule* and *Ulster will Fight and Ulster will be Right.*

The Irish Republican Brotherhood had meanwhile been busy infiltrating other Irish organisations that had grown up in the closing years of the nineteenth century: the Gaelic League – reviving Ireland's language, legends, poetry and culture – the Gaelic Athletic Association and Sinn Fein. This entryism allowed the terrorists to select and train the essential revolutionary cell. With Ulster being stirred to rabidry, a National Volunteer Force sprang up in response in the south. The IRB infiltrated this too, taking over its leadership and training.

When the First World War broke out, the nationalists split, the majority calling off the struggle for the duration, along with Redmond's parliamentary party. The minority, on the principle that England's difficulty was Ireland's opportunity, stuck to their revolutionary path, though they were also, as ever, split. Padraic Pearse, a poet, leader of the militants, wanted a rising even if it failed like all the rest, because IRB philosophy envisaged that eventually, after one more bloody rising, the people would be shamed out of their lethargy. On 24 April 1916, the day after Easter Sunday, Pearse, as C-in-C of Irish forces, proclaimed the Irish Republic from the steps of Dublin's General Post Office; Pearse was named president of the provisional government; James Connolly as vice-president and commander of all rebel forces in Dublin. In the ensuing fighting between the Irish forces and British troops over 1300 people were killed or seriously wounded, and Pearse and Connolly agreed to an unconditional surrender, on 30 April, only to avoid further deaths. Of the ninety rebels condemned to death, fifteen were executed, making them instant martyrs. A wave of revulsion swept the country, aided by W.B. Yeats's fine poem Easter 1916 and Lloyd George's blunders. Irish political support deserted the official Irish Home Rule MPs in favour of the new Independence party, Sinn Fein – which had played no part in the Easter Rising. Count Plunkett, father of Joseph Plunkett, one of the executed rebels, and Éamonn de Valera, who had been reprieved from execution on account of his youth, won by-elections. Lloyd George's introduction of conscription put the non-political farmers into the opposition camp, whilst the arrest of Sinn Fein leaders allowed Michael Collins, who escaped, to take over leadership of the party. Despite the arrests, Sinn Fein won 73 out of 103 seats in the 1918 general election, on a programme of outright republican separation. Approximately half of these MPs were in prison, but the remainder – except for Ulster Unionists – set themselves up as a constituent assembly in Dublin in January 1921. De Valera, in prison, was elected President.

The Liberal government's answer to this was neither new nor Liberal: coercion and repression. Auxillary policemen, the Black-and-Tans, composed largely of hardened ex-servicemen, were recruited to reinforce the hard-pressed

constabulary, which then proceeded in traditional Tudor style to spread fear, mayhem and hatred of the British indiscriminately throughout the country. They made potential allies into implacable enemies in record time and sparked off a full-scale civil war (1919–21) in which the military organisation of Michael Collins effectively blocked the British army. By 1921, Lloyd George realised that neither the British public nor the United States would stand for repression of the Irish much longer. Truce talks were held, in which the cunning and unscrupulous Liberal Prime Minister used the threat of total war to secure the best terms he could. The Irish Free State emerged, Ireland without six Ulster counties, with British naval bases and Dominion status, like Canada, independent but acknowledging allegiance to the King.

This was not an Irish Republic, and it split the Irish. A general election confirmed the deal, but de Valera, as sole heir of the men of the Easter Rising, repudiated it. A second and terrible civil war (1922–3) ensued, a time of bloody executions, murders, fanatical destruction of great houses and beautiful buildings. The revolution destroyed its own children: Collins, Erskine Childers, Rory O'Connor, Liam Mellows, and others. The new government had to be more ruthless than the British to survive. Eventually, in 1923, de Valera called off armed resistance. The hatreds have lasted, but it was hardly to be expected that a free Ireland, conceived in the horror and misery of the Famine could be born without bloodshed and suffering.

By the 1927 elections, de Valera and most of his republicans had come to terms with the reality, taken an oath of allegiance and become MPs in the Dail. The extremists broke away, founded the IRA and became a small, unpopular

underground movement. De Valera became Prime Minister in 1932, sparked off a British trade embargo, imposed high tariffs on British goods and set about an economic and industrial development programme. He also changed the country's name to Eire (which means Ireland and doesn't imply the existence of Ulster), and in ending the trade war in 1938 got Britain to withdraw its naval bases. Like Portugal and Spain, Ireland stayed neutral in the Second World War: it could hardly have done otherwise. There was no conscription in Northern Ireland for fear of Catholic reaction, but many thousands of Irishmen served in British regiments. Most of the IRA spent the war in either British or Irish gaols. The declaration of the independent Republic by de Valera's successor, John Costello, in 1948, cut links that had already atrophied, but it also caused the Labour government to formally guarantee continuing British support for the North, due mainly to the big part they had played in the war.

The Republic is a country with inbred problems. The great revival of Irish culture and Gaelic has not continued, despite a lot of effort. The Catholic Church, which runs education, no more runs Ireland than it runs Italy. Its influence appears to be less now than it was in colonial days: the priest has achieved middle class status and no longer shares the poverty of the peasant. Unemployment and emigration, including emigration to Northern Ireland, remain despite a great deal of effort to stem them. De Valera's industrialisation was not really successful though nationalised industries have done reasonably well, such as the Peat Board, Tourist Board and Aer Lingus. Agriculture is still fairly backward and far below potential, again despite much government effort. Membership of the EEC and the economic policies introduced by Sean Lemass in the 1960s have made her a more attractive proposition for foreign investment. Euro-finance is helping to modernise agriculture, and, as in Portugal, rich Europeans are buying up the old estates, mansions and castles.

The problem of Ulster, the chance creation of Lloyd George, has worsened since the late 1960s. The IRA, moribund by the Fifties, emerged in the Sixties with new vigour, new political orientation towards the extreme left and a new funding from naïve, sentimental Americans and crackpot Eastern dictators. In parts of Belfast and Derry, No-Go areas established by riot and weekly reprisals are IRA enclaves: areas along the border with the Republic are very unsafe. Growing dialogue between the two governments is a sign of possible hope, but intransigent opposition to any London–Dublin accord continues to be vigorous in the North – and in some sections of the Conservative party. Ultimately, the IRA would appear to be counting on the British public becoming so sickened by the bloodshed and the cost of security that a future government would, like Lloyd George of old, cut and run. Perhaps, however, European federalism might provide a new answer to this very old problem.

taly

The Romans of antiquity were, arguably, quite the most impressive people ever to grace the Continent of Europe. They were serious, persevering and moral, building their power laboriously on discipline, hard work and aggression; without them Europe would probably have remained like Africa, a continent of warring tribes and not much else.

The Italians, however, are not modern descendants of the Romans, as Mussolini found to his cost. As the original Latin Rome expanded, it absorbed Etruscans, Greeks, Gauls, people from all over Europe and beyond who came into the Empire as subjects, slaves, merchants and soldiers. After the Empire collapsed whole nations of Teutons swarmed in – Goths from Germany, Lombards from Scandinavia – and from then on till the creation of the modern Italian state in 1871, Italy was perpetually under foreign occupation, by Byzantines, Arabs, Normans, Spaniards, Germans, French and Austrians.

HE'S RIGHT OF COURSE. THE TIDES CAN BE VERY DANGEROUS IN MARCH.

So Italians, virtuous though they be, are definitely not Romans. They aren't even particularly keen on being Italians, regarding themselves still primarily as Sicilians, Florentines, Sienese or whatever.

Naturally, even the Romans could become decadent, though this aspect of their Empire has been grossly exaggerated by divers bitchy little writers from Suetonius to the Fathers of the Church. Such scribes and pharisees have highlighted the freaks and monsters like Elagabalus and Commodus at the expense of a great number of excellent, typically Roman emperors and generals who continued to give of their best in very difficult circumstances right up to and beyond The End. The century of the Antonines – AD 96 to AD 190 – was the Empire's Golden Age: Nerva, Trajan, Hadrian, Antoninus Pius and Marcus Aurelius. Thereafter, things fell apart as the will of the people to continue to deal with provincial rebellions and barbarian incursions became sapped by easy vices and cheap thrills. Ambition and greed weakened the system. The Emperor Aurelian (270–275) ordered all cities to be walled: a clear indication that the Dark Ages were on their way. Diocletian (284–305) and Constantine (306–337) divided the Empire to make the parts more governable and defensible, moving the capital to Ravenna, and in the East, to Constantinople. The basic problems remained: too many needy and desperate barbarians pushing in from Eastern Europe and beyond. The decline became a fall in 410. It was all very much like today.

It was the legacy of the Empire – the administrative framework, the civil service and the Church – that allowed the rude fragmentary tribal kingdoms of Dark

O MY GOD! IT'S NOT JUST ANOTHER WILD PARTY THEN?

Age Europe to become nation states, yet Italy, paradoxically, was to remain in fragments till modern times whilst even Scotland, that had no imperial legacy, had the makings of a nation by the eleventh century. Partly this was due to attitude: the belief that, having created Europe singlehandedly out of bog and oak forests, any serious political effort after 410 AD – either their own or anyone else's – should be treated with cynicism and contempt. Partly it was due to accidents of history: for example, the Italian conquests of Justinian, Charlemagne, the Saracens and the Normans all split the country into a Continental north and a Mediterranean south – a split that has gone on till the present time. And partly it was due to the rise and rise of the Roman Catholic papacy, which for many hundreds of years channelled off a high proportion of the likely lads, visionaries and gangsters, who should have been otherwise employed helping some ambitious noble establish a kingdom.

The Church had already taken over the religious life of the Empire by Constantine's time, using a versatile mix of bigotry, forgeries and pogroms. Pope Gregory the Great, late sixth century, countered the advance of the Lombards by establishing the Papal States right across central Italy from Rome to Ravenna: the Church held onto these for thirteen hundred years. Its vigour waned: scandalous Popes occurred with embarrassing frequency – including children and at least one lady. Pope Leo III saved his own bacon by the fortuitous crowning of Charlemagne in 800, a cynical revival of the old imperial ideal which gave substance to the Church's claim to be able to make and unmake temporal sovereigns. It also, alas, brought in ambitious German Holy

Roman Emperors, such as Otto the Great in 966, whose claims to rule Italy brought them into increasing conflict with reviving, reforming and expansionist Popes. From the time of Pope Gregory VII onwards from 1073, a centralised European papacy was in being and growing ever stronger, claiming universal supremacy over all monarchies – a claim backed up by a very convincing forgery, the Donation of Constantine. Urban II increased the scope further by initiating the Crusades in 1095, while Innocent III (1198–1215) nearly succeeded in establishing complete papal theocracy, his power extending like a medieval Domitian's even to far-off England. In Italy this meant continual holy or temporal warfare between Popes and any Holy Roman Emperors (i.e. Germans), or their allies powerful enough to dispute papal power. Rival parties – Guelphs (for Papacy and people) and Ghibellines (for Emperor and nobles) – battled it out in every corner of the country in innumerable insurrections, battles and invasions.

These divisions allowed the rise of the commercial republics such as Venice, Genoa and Pisa, thereby providing neutral and increasingly prosperous enclaves and making Italy an essential part of medieval commerce. Merchants from all over the Continent came to them for the coveted products of the East. The privileges they obtained from Constantinople and the Holy Land put the Mediterranean in their hands as the Byzantines ceased to dominate it. Their wars were, like their commerce, strictly professional, conducted by *condottieri* who knew neither feudal loyalty nor national sentiment, and like most wars they brought tyrants to power, as in Milan, Ferrara and Padua. In the south, always following a different pattern, the Saracens were followed by Normans, by the German Hohenstaufen who were scuppered by the papacy and replaced by the French, who, following the Sicillian Vespers of 1282, had to give way to the House of Aragon.

By the fourteenth century the papacy, relying on French support, had already become too big for its own boots. From 1305 to 1377 it took itself off to Avignon where it busied itself with French politics as it had previously done with Italian. The Great Schism that followed (1377–1417), a period when there were rival Popes in Rome and Avignon, further discredited it at a time when the Italian states and cities were establishing an intellectual supremacy in Europe based on the reawakening of interest in the classical world and its values, itself the result of trade with Byzantium and the East. Medievalism was in full-scale retreat and the papacy was seen as no more than another powerful principality. Princely houses such as the Gonzaga, Visconti, Sforza and de Medici struggled to be at the front of this Renaissance, and their citizens warmly applauded their efforts in securing or patronising the works of Donatello, Michelangelo, Bramante, Leonardo da Vinci, Raphael, Titian, Correggio, Palestrina, Vivaldi and so many more great artists of the fifteenth and sixteenth centuries that Italy was indeed like a re-born Ancient Greece, the well from which all Europe came to drink, the well from which countless heavy, ox-like princes and noblemen's sons returned northwards to their foggy, forested fastnesses, realising dimly for the first time that it was no longer enough for a nobleman just to wield a sword or a battle-axe. And,

IMBECILE!
NOW IT'LL NEVER BE
FINISHED. YOU GAVE HIM
THE DUCHESS'S
GOBLET.

though the works of Niccolò Machiavelli and the country's long practice of the arts of diplomacy and political subtlety made Italy the teacher of statecraft to the sovereigns of Europe, she remained, like Ancient Greece, disunited, the tempting prey to powerful foreign invaders.

Great as this Renaissance was in its effects on Europe, the most effective Renaissance man of all was a seaman, one Christopher Columbus, reputedly from Genoa. His chance discovery – several centuries after the Vikings – of the New World ended Italy's centrality to the old one, and from 1492 onwards, slowly but inevitably, the Mediterranean became a backwater as the peripheral Atlantic powers – Spain, Portugal, France, England and the Netherlands – grew ever richer on the trade and plunder. The triumph of the Turks in the eastern Mediterranean contributed to Italy's economic eclipse.

The sixteenth century saw France and Spain expanding vigorously, both of them pushing claims to large chunks of Italy. The country was invaded again and again as they fought it out, the greater states – the Duchies of Milan and Savoy, the Republics of Venice, Florence and Siena – held apart by their continuing rivalries, the lesser ones becoming pawns for the two rivals. In the end, the Habsburgs proved too much for the French, the Emperor Charles V sacked Rome, and by the Treaty of Cateau-Cambresis, 1559, all Italy fell under Spanish Habsburg dominance and remained under for the rest of the sixteenth and seventeenth centuries. As in Flanders, it was not a pleasant or productive experience. Lombardy, Naples and Sicily were ruled by Spanish viceroys who, with their numerous subordinates treated the opportunity as a

NICE PICTURE, YES,
BUT IT'S HARDLY THE
DUKE IS IT?

God-given ticket to get rich. The native population, especially in the south, declined into lethargy; so did Venice and Florence, although the Papal States expanded as Counter-Reformation Popes sharpened up their act in response to Protestantism.

In all this long decline into lethargy, corruption and foreign exploitation, there appears to have been no stirring of revolution. The poor continued, apparently, to derive endless satisfaction from the ostentation of their nobles. In Naples, the largest city at this time, there were 100 princes and 150 dukes, living, as elsewhere, in palazzi with fancy baroque facades set in squalid streets, often penuriously empty save for a few furnished upstairs rooms. Servants in fine livery, ornate carriages, gondolas and fabulous entertainments came first: to maintain such outward show, noble families denied themselves almost everything else. Only eldest sons were allowed to marry, the others going into the bosom of mother Church.

When revolution did come it was as a foreign import, brought by Napoleon. At first the Italians were intrigued with the notions of Liberty, Equality and Fraternity, but when it became clear that their liberators really meant Blood, Sweat and Discipline, they found them more oppressive than their old masters, and Napoleon's innovations – puppet republics, a Kingdom of Italy in the north and the Papal States overrun – vanished as soon as the great Liberator was out of the way. The peace settlement of 1815 left Austria in almost complete control of the peninsula: Venice and Lombardy under their direct control, Tuscany, Modena and Parma under other Habsburgs, Piedmont and Naples basically relying on Austrian support against any stirrings of revolution. Throughout

THAT'S ANOTHER OF YOUR
GENUINE ETRUSCAN URNS
GONE, LUIGI.

GRAND TOU
REPRODUCTIONS

Europe it was an era of rigid reactionary governments, all of them determined to support each other against anything remotely resembling outbreaks of Jacobinism. As elsewhere, however, the Napoleonic shock administered to an old, enervated and stifling system introduced a virus that was to prove fatal in the end: nationalism.

Like all the ideals of the French Revolution, nationalism was a bourgeois phenomenon, appealing to the urban, idealistic young of the slightly more than downtrodden classes, which account for its many unsuccessful revolts in the face of thoroughgoing repression. It accounts also for its masonic secret societies, like the Carbonari, out of which Giuseppe Mazzini, a Genoese lawyer, founded the Young Italy movement in the 1830s. It also accounts for the fact that Count Cavour, a Piedmontese aristocrat, decided in the end that he could use nationalism – as Prince Bismarck did in Germany – to establish his reluctant monarch on the throne of a new, nationalistic kingdom of Italy. It does not however account for Guiseppe Garibaldi, a seaman from Nice – then in Italy – who met Mazzini in Marseilles and was much impressed by the ideals of Young Italy. Straightway he became a republican revolutionary and went off to Brazil to learn the trade, joining the rebels against the unfortunate Emperor there, marrying a beautiful creole, escaping from torture and returning to Europe just in time for the Year of Revolutions (1848).

Curiously, Italy's contributions to this event were a sparked off by the unlikely figure of Pope Pius IX, whom the Roman populace mistakenly regarded as a liberal. In fact, he was a dither. Mass demonstrations led to Austrian occupation

of the papal city of Ferrara. King Ferdinand of Naples' subjects rose against him, proclaiming a British-style constitution. The Venetians rose against the Austrians and drove out their governor, Marshal Radetzky, in five days of non-stop fighting. Despite the promptings of Cavour, King Charles Albert of Savoy vacillated, then stepped in and was beaten by Radetzky. In Rome, Pope Pius having fled, a republic was proclaimed under Mazzini, Garibaldi arriving to defend it with a few thousand 'Redshirts'. The Pope appealed to the Catholic powers to restore him, the French sent in an army and Garibaldi held it at bay, to the wonder of Europe, for three months, after which, the city having capitulated, he went to help the Venetians who were still holding out against Radetzky. Three Austrian armies as well as the victorious troops of King Ferdinand hunted Garibaldi down through the mountains till he eventually escaped – his wife having died in these escapades – via San Marino to the United States.

Ten years of dire repression followed. Radetzky taxed Lombardy and Venetia to starvation. In Naples, 4000 were condemned for political crimes and executed or rotted in gaols. In Rome, unscrupulous and reactionary cardinals held sway. Mazzini died in exile.

And there it might have ended had it not been for Count Cavour, who with his new master King Victor Emmanuel II saw the possibility of expanding Savoy over the whole peninsula if he could find a cheap way of uniting people in their hatred of the Austrians and their allies. They set about expanding their army with volunteers from all over Italy. Garibaldi returned and pledged his support. 'Italy and Victor Emmanuel' was their catch-phrase. Then Cavour pulled off a diplomatic coup after much hoodwinking and horse-trading with Napoleon III whereby the French were to help drive the Austrians out of Venetia and Lombardy. Getting wind of this, the Austrians forthwith invaded Piedmont (1859) and Garibaldi held them off till the French got there. The Austrians were defeated at San Martino and Solferino, but at that point Napoleon, ever the gambler, jacked it in, considering a united Italy would be a worse neighbour than the reactionary Austrians. This forced Victor Emmanuel to make peace, and Cavour resigned in disgust.

He still believed, however, that he was on a winner. In 1860 Garibaldi sailed with a thousand Redshirts in two creaking steamers for Sicily. They had no fuel, no food, no ammunition, and they badly needed engine repairs. Some ships of the Royal Navy gave some cover, but all the odds – and a Neapolitan army of 30,000 – were against Garibaldi. This, nevertheless, was the spark that finally set all the old timber aflame, as Cavour had hoped. The Garibaldini swept up through Italy from the south to howls of protest from all reactionary European powers, and would certainly have swept through the Papal States as well if Cavour hadn't patched up an emergency scheme with France to forestall them, in case a Garibaldi takeover caused a Catholic European crusade into Italy in 1861. So Garibaldi greeted Victor Emmanuel at the border and hailed him as King of Italy, and His Majesty saw to it that the hero of the nation was rapidly shipped off to the island of Caprera and the Redshirts disbanded before they could cause any more embarrassment. The last thing Cavour wanted was real revolution. In 1866, as a result of their defeat by Prussia, the Austrians handed over Venetia, and in 1871, following another Prussian victory, over France, the French protecting army left Rome, the Pope took himself off to the Vatican, and the Papal States ceased to exist. For the first time in nearly 1600 years, Italy was one country and Rome once again a capital.

It had been great theatre, and had the curtain gone down there for the last time it would have merited round after round of rapturous applause. The sequel was not really a success: a northern, businessman's bourgeois kingdom, with an unstable parliamentary structure, industrialisation, hot air politics and graft. As ineffective coalition governments came and went, a violent Socialist movement sprang up outside parliament which did for King Umberto in 1900. Only massive emigration as organgrinders and ice-cream men helped the south. From these millions, hard-earned dollars and pounds trickled back to help poverty-stricken families survive. Such people were hardly enamoured of the benefits of parliamentary democracy, nationalism and unification. Nor were the old nobility and landowners when northern carpet-baggers emerged as the parvenus of the new kingdom. Not till 1904 did the Pope allow Catholics to vote, and then only in order to keep out the Socialists. After a lot of blood, toil, sweat and tears, the new nation acquired some rather undesirable colonial possessions: Eritrea, bits of Somaliland and Libya. They were thrashed by ill-equipped Abyssinians at the Battle of Adowa, 1896, and denied any share of the more profitable bits of North Africa by France. In the First World War they were routed by the Austrians at Caporetto (1917) whilst at the ensuing Peace they acquired South Tyrol and Istria, but not half as much as they had been promised by politicians such as Lloyd George. Discontented ex-servicemen, rapidly rising costs of living as well as industrial and social unrest were further benefits. The politicians proved inept and unscrupulous nonentities – and fear of Bolshevism was their sole obvious policy. Benito Mussolini's rise to power from 1919 to 1922 was therefore rapid: he alone offered dramatic answers to all the problems. The Italians are an operatic people. Garibaldi had been pure Verdi. Mussolini was the Italians' answer to Gilbert and Sullivan.

Yet the inventor of Fascism – he derived some of it from d'Annunzio, post-war dictator of Fiume – was basically a gifted demagogue who succeeded for a while in providing the most popular government United Italy has ever had. Mussolini had spent his preparatory years casting around for a power base, and after the war with so many alienated groups – Socialists, the South, the nobility, the Church – it was unsurprising that his coup d'etat 'The March on Rome' (he went by train actually) succeeded. His regime provided a lot of things that had been lacking in Italy since unification: theatricality, the *bella figura*, grandiose vision, national pride and the involvement of all classes in the nation's progress. Trains ran on time, autostrada were built, marshes were drained, 57 per cent of government income was spent on the South. He reached a peak of popularity in 1929 with his Concordat with the Papacy, which restored the traditional place of the Catholic Church in Italy, recognised the Vatican City State and secured the support of Catholics for the regime. In theory it was totalitarian, but in comparison with Germany, the USSR or with Britain during the Second World War it was far from that, Italians being one of the least likely of peoples to accept regimentation

AND IT ISN'T JUST THE TRAINS YOU KNOW. HIS HOLINESS HIMSELF IS A LOT MORE PUNCTUAL.

for the good of the state. The Church, the army, the monarchy and business all retained considerable autonomy. Mussolini's state wore an ugly face and fascist gangs beat up their opponents, but they used doses of castor oil as punishment rather than extermination camps or knee-capping. The bureaucracy remained far too inefficient to run anything seriously lethal.

However, as his various grandiose schemes slowly fell apart and he began to lose popularity, Il Duce turned to the traditional vote-catcher, foreign conquest. The Abyssinian War, 1935–6, gave him some glory and deluded some Italians into belief that Imperial Rome was on the march again, but from 1937 onwards he fell under the influence of Hitler. Further foreign adventures, in Albania and Greece, were big mistakes and his role in the Second World War disastrous: a third of the army was overseas, it was still equipped with 1891 rifles and World War One artillery, and less than a third of the Duce's aeroplanes were in a fit state to fly. The Italians didn't want war and the increasing role of the Germans in their country reawakened nasty memories of centuries of Germanic invasion and domination. Following heavy defeats in North Africa and with Allied invasion imminent, Mussolini was deposed, imprisoned, daringly rescued by German parachutists in 1943, recaptured, then finally shot and hanged by partisans in April 1945.

Italy in 1945 was at its lowest ebb since the Dark Ages. Its reputation and resources had been sorely depleted, vast modern armies had fought every inch of the way up through the country from Sicily, destroying towns, villages, bridges, monasteries and other relics of previous, more advanced, civilizations. Partisans,

BUT OF COURSE IT WAS BUILT LIKE THAT SIGNORA. WHO WOULD COME TO PISA IF IT WAS STRAIGHT?

mainly Communists, roamed freely settling old scores and private feuds. All overseas possessions were lost, as were frontier areas to France and Yugoslavia. Politically it was impossible to see what should be done. By a tiny majority, a plebiscite voted for a republic. The Allies saw to it that the constitution and its PR system would prevent fascists taking over again, but the dismal record of pre-1922 parliamentarianism gave little hope for the future. The US gave considerable generous aid.

Rapid industrialization, helped by the discovery of oil and gas, followed in the Fifties and Sixties. Cars, fashions, films, furnishings, chemicals, ships, machinery and tourism have supplemented traditional agricultural exports, pollution and inflation being serious problems. A determined governmental effort has been made to develop the South, including land reclamation, water and electricity schemes and development grants – as in the Scottish Highlands. And, as in the Highlands, unemployment and emigration to industrial regions continue endemic, though the Highlands don't have the Mafia. (They do, however, have MacLeods.) Crime, like pollution, is a vigorous growth.

Politically, Italy remains unstable, with violence and extremism erupting from time to time, as in the Red Brigades of the 1970s. There have been fifty governments since the Second World War, at the last count, most of them dominated by the Catholic, Christian Democratic, party, though the Communists have been the strongest single unit and control many of the local governments. The Church remains powerful in the lives of the people, though the feminist movement is challenging its attitudes on various matters. Like the Belgians, whose history since the Dark Ages has been rather similar, the Italians are supreme political cynics, having been ruled and overrun by just about everyone. They mistrust all officials, and regard laws, rules and regulations as challenging obstacles to be circumvented by the exercise of their considerable native ingenuity. Above all, they know the utter futility of war, which is probably why they are among the foremost advocates of a united Western Europe.

Luxemburg

The Grand Duchy of Luxemburg has a population of some 355,000, and occupies a land area not much bigger than that of Caithness. In the Middle Ages it was four times its present size, when some of its more ambitious Counts were also Holy Roman Emperors, their writ running, in theory at least, from the North Sea to Muscovy, from the Baltic to the Alps. It has also, like Belgium next door, been conquered and dominated for hundreds of years by neighbours with vastly greater resources, so that resistance has been a national pastime since Roman times. The national motto, *'Mir woelle bleiwe wat mir sin'* – in Letzeburgesch, a distinct Germanic tongue – meaning 'We want to remain what we are' sums it all up.

The Romans had a hard fight on their hands moving in here against the Celts, particularly in the face of frequent revolts backed by Druids. Unusually for the Romans, druidism was a proscribed religion in the empire, though they never succeeded in stamping it out in Luxemburg, where it

IT'S ALL RIGHT, MARCUS.
HE'S WHAT THEY CALL AN
ARDENNES HAM.

may yet lurk. Ardennes ham and Moselle wines were the main exports to Rome.

Attila the Hun came through here on his way to the Battle of Chalons, 451, and the Luxemburgers were impressed enough to name one of their Roman bridges after him, Ettelbruck. Various confused barbarian incursions followed Attila's defeat, the Franks soon afterwards dominating the rest. Missionaries pushed their way through the forests and fastnesses, St Willibrord from Northumbria founding a monastery here around AD 700. When Charlemagne created his new Roman Empire, Luxemburg received a thousand Saxon families to populate its Ardennes region – and partly because Charlemagne, like Stalin, moved populations around to prevent them giving more trouble. On the breakup of this effort, Luxemburg became part of Lotharingia, and was soon, like all the other parts, submerged in the general welter of Dark Age mayhem from which feudalism was the only way out. In a charter of 963, the Abbey of St Maximin of Trier granted to Sigefroi or Siegfried, Count of the Ardennes, lands that included the strategic ruined Roman fort of *Castellum Lucilinburhuc*, and thus named, Luxemburg burst upon an astonished world. Sigefroi and his successors used their strong right arms and heavy swords to establish a town and county they called Lützelburg.

The fortunes of the House of Lützelburg rose and fell. William (1096–1128) was the first officially styled Count of Luxemburg. From their fortress town on a rock above a ravine, and from their castles in the Ardennes his successors extended the feudal domains. Luxemburg knights went with Godfrey of Bouillon to Jerusalem on the First Crusade. Luxemburg barons took up crusading as

a major sport, selling off and gambling away their fiefs to raise the necessary funds for their journey, or leaving them to be mismanaged, debt-ridden, in their prolonged absences.

By the time Count Henry the Blind died in 1196, there wasn't much left of Luxemburg, and what there was was within the grasp of the German Hohenstaufens. Henry left a minor as heir, a daughter, so it looked as if they were about to join the German Empire in complete obscurity like several thousand other feudal territories. Countess Ermesinde (1196–1247) had other ideas. She married Theobald of Bar, a descendant of Sigefroi's father, Wigerik, and he won back all the territory and added more. When he died, Ermesinde, then eighteen, took to her bosom Waleran of Limburg, who added more still. On Waleran's demise in 1225, she herself took over the government. She re-established Luxemburg's prestige and vigorously centralised the state by taking power from feudal functionaries, by issuing charters to towns and bringing them under her direct authority, by extending rights of justice to burghers, and by removing feudal restrictions on movement and liberty. She established schools, convents and other cultural centres. She made Luxemburg into a modern nation before modern nations existed, her efforts, and her husbands' endeavours, creating a prosperous state in an advantageous strategic position in the heart of Western Europe.

Wisely or unwisely, her successors in the fourteenth and fifteenth centuries chose to use Ermesinde's legacy as a springboard to their attempts to dominate Europe. In 1308, Henry Count of Luxemburg was elected Holy Roman Emperor

(Henry VII) by the judicious use of bribes and the efforts of two of the electors who just happened to be Luxemburgers. His son, John, Count of Luxemburg and King of Bohemia (1310–46), was a great and famous courtly knight of the high Middle Ages – already slightly anachronistic – who battled his way for thirty years all over Europe from the Baltic to the Po, from the Carpathians to Crécy, where, already blind, he lost his life. It was from John – a Luxemburg hero to this day – that the English Black Prince copied the three ostrich feathers and motto '*Ich Dien*' ('I serve') which have since become known in England as the Prince of Wales's feathers.

John's son, the Emperor Charles IV (1347–78), and two of his successors, Wenceslas (Emperor, 1378–1400) and Sigismund (Emperor, 1410–38), worked long and hard, and increasingly in despair, to make something workable out of the Holy Roman German Empire, but it too was an anachronism, its powers and chief financial resources long since bartered away. Within six years of Sigismund's death, Luxemburg had lost its independence and its dynasty, swallowed by the growing power of Burgundy, a power that Sigismund had allowed to go unchecked as he swanned about Europe from England to Hungary on doomed and stillborn imperial business.

And thus it remained for nearly 400 years, first a province of Burgundy, then of the powers which reaped in turn the Burgundian inheritance: Spain, France and Austria. Because of its strategic position its independence was not to be contemplated, its capital was turned into one of the greatest fortresses in Europe, much of the fortification being the work of Vauban, the great

BLIND HE MAY BE,
GODFREY, BUT HE KNOWS
HOW TO WIELD A
WHITE STICK.

military engineer of Louis XIV. It was, they said, the 'fortress at the fulcrum of Europe'.

One beneficial result of the French Revolution and the Napoleonic Wars – there weren't many – was the final flushing out of the Austrian Habsburgs from Luxemburg and Belgium next door. The Congress of Vienna (1815) had to turn its attention to the question of who was now to govern these territories which for so long had been under foreign domination. In Luxemburg's case they came up with the sort of solution characteristic of the nineteenth century: the eastern part of the territory was given to Prussia, the remainder was declared an independent Grand Duchy, the Grand Duke was to be William, King of the Netherlands, but the Grand Duchy was not to be incorporated into the Dutch state but, instead, was to be part of the German Confederation set up by the Congress, and a Prussian army was to occupy the capital for fifty-two years. Following the revolt of Belgium from Dutch rule and the subsequent invasion by King William, a further restructuring took place in 1839, when more than half of William's territory was given to Belgium, where it forms the Belgian province of Luxemburg to this day. The Grand Duchy's independence and neutrality were guaranteeed anew by the Powers, but the Dutch King remained Grand Duke, and the Prussian garrison stayed too. At yet another conference, in London, in 1867, the Grand Duchy was declared 'a free state, independent and indivisible': in return for dismantling Vauban's mighty fortress, she was allowed to leave the German Confederation – just in time to avoid being smothered in Bismarck's Reich – whereafter the normally undemonstrative Luxemburgers were observed dancing and singing in the streets. In 1890, her link with the Dutch was finally severed when Queen Wilhelmina became Queen there and Adolf of Orange-Nassau became Grand Duke of Luxemburg.

At the start of the nineteenth century, Luxemburg had been a backwater, an impoverished agricultural territory exhausted by other people's wars and scarcely able to feed itself; thousands emigrated. Then it was discovered that fine steel could be made from the iron-ore deposits in the south by using newly invented English processes. Even more fortunately, it was discovered that the wastes from the smelting were exactly the sort of fertiliser required for the soil of the north and central farmlands. Prosperity followed.

In the First World War, 3000 died fighting with the Allies. A plebiscite at the end of it, on the abdication of the Grand Duchess Marie-Adelaide, confirmed overwhelming support for her successor Charlotte rather than for a republic. In 1921 a customs and economic treaty with Belgium, forerunner of the Benelux union after the Second World War, facilitated the return of prosperity. In the Second World War, it took the Nazis only a few hours during May 1940 to overrun the territory, yet there was considerable resistance, and many men joined other anti-German armies. When the Nazis imposed military conscription to the Wehrmacht, the Luxemburgers refused, went on strike and nailed their red, white and blue flag to factory masts. Savage reprisals followed.

As war again rolled across the diminutive Duchy, including the Battle of the Bulge and von Runstedt's Offensive, 35 per cent of the farmland could not be tilled, 60,000 homes were ruined, 160 bridges and tunnels were destroyed, railways and rolling-stock disappeared into the Reich, over half the roads were blown up or bombed into impassability and steel plants became burnt out with over-production for Germany. Some 10,000 US servicemen and some 11,000 Germans are buried in Luxemburg.

'*Mir woelle bleiwe wat mir sin*': a dogged sense of purpose, solidarity and hard work are the virtues of Luxemburgers and the tiny country recovered in an amazingly short time from the devastation of modern war. With Belgium and the Netherlands she was among the first to see the paramount importance thenceforward of European co-operation. She was in the Benelux union in 1948, the Coal & Steel Community in 1950, the EEC in 1957. She is the home of the secretariat of the European Parliament, seat of the Court of Justice and the European Investment Bank, and for three months every year the Council of Ministers of the EC meet there.

Netherlands

If ever there was proof of the Baron de Montesquieu's contention that the characteristics of a nation are the product of its geography and climate, it's the Dutch. From time immemorial they have clung, to the incredulity of their neighbours, to a land that Nature has long intended to be part of the sea-bed. Their earliest ancestors had to erect mounds of earth and wicker on which to survive, as the cold, foggy waters of the North Sea and the great rivers Rhine, Maas and Scheldt lapped ever more urgently about their cold and rheumy shanks. They have been fighting the sea twenty-four hours a day ever since, losing 566,580 hectares of land to it in the last eight centuries yet also gaining 687,900. Their struggle can never be won, but it has made the Dutch dour enough to go on fighting, and ingenious enough to have made their enemy their highway to the riches that their bogs and pastures almost wholly lack. The Dutch have other characteristics: 2000 thousand years of

THERE'S NO DOUBT ABOUT IT, PIET. WE'RE LOOKING AT THE SHAPE OF THE FUTURE.

living on man-made mounds cheek by jowl with one's fellow humans fosters tolerance.

Caesar conquered the Belgae next door. The Batavians of central Holland were thereafter subjugated and Romanised, but the Frisians of the north remained largely unaffected by civilisation of any sort, safe from envy and exploitation in their foggy damp. They also escaped Frankish domination, allying themselves with the neighbouring Saxons for this purpose and thereby remaining heathens till converted by St Willibrord from Northumbria in the eighth century. As if in retribution, the old gods unleashed the Dark Ages, which meant, as elsewhere, that everything got worse: seaborne Vikings and other murderers, robbers and slave-masters plundered them for 200 years.

Here as elsewhere, Feudalism was the answer. Castles, inhabited by counts, were built at the mouths of the rivers, and fortified towns sprang up in their protection. Charlemagne, Lotharingia and various dynasties came and went, even if little of it affected the Dutch or helped their daily struggle. Most of their counts owed allegiance to the Holy Roman Empire with the exception of the Count of Flanders in the south who was nominally a vassal of the French King. The Frisians acknowledged no overlords, and spoke a language of their own devising.

Medieval civilisation developed and in 1271, the Count of Holland founded Amsterdam. Dutch ingenuity transformed the primitive wooden towns into centres of industry, commerce and sea-borne prosperity, many of these towns being virtually independent republics. Their growing importance and potential,

and the benefits of controlling the three great rivers was perceived by the powerful. The Dukes of Burgundy, heirs of Lotharingia, moved in on the land of bog and clog. Philip the Bold acquired Flanders in 1384. His grandson, Philip the Fair, acquired Holland, Zealand and other parts. Philip's son Charles continued the process. They centralised government, summoned provincial delegates to a States General, raised an army and imposed taxes. A ducal representative, the Stadtholder, was appointed as provincial governor in each province.

The Dutch resented it: they had made the land and made its towns prosperous entirely by their own toil, and now they were having to pay rich foreigners for the privilege. When Duke Charles was killed at the famous Battle of Nancy (1477) the States General forced his successor, his daughter Mary, to sign the 'Great Privilege', which reasserted provincial liberties. However, when Mary married Maximilian of Austria it soon became clear to the Dutch that they had lost: the Habsburgs were taking over just about everywhere in the known and unknown world, and Holland was merely a tiny part of their multinational enterprise. With the accession of the Emperor Charles V in 1519, even the gallant Frisians were added to the legacies of Burgundy, Spain and the Holy Roman Empire. The land became known as the Seven United Provinces.

Charles centralised the Low Countries – the Netherlands and Belgium – as a unit, freeing them from direct imperial control as a concession. The Dutch and the Belgians, however, were not and never have been a unit. Blunt Dutch burghers resented French-speaking Stadtholders and their fancy courtiers. Worse than that, they were Catholics, the Dutch having in the meantime switched to Protestantism, a dourer form of religion. Charles, a moderate despite being lumbered with the responsibility for championing the Catholic Church, managed to prevent religious civil war, but only just; conflict broke out all over Germany.

His successor, Philip II, King of Spain (1556–98), was a Catholic bigot with a rigid Spanish style. Taking himself off permanently to Madrid, he gave orders on departing for all prominent Calvinists – as a dourer form of protestant – to be brought before the Inquisition. The functionary who received this order was William, Prince of Orange-Nassau, nicknamed 'The Silent' as he had worked his way up the promotion ladder under Charles and Philip by keeping his ears open and his mouth shut. William was both a secret Protestant and a gifted opportunist: the Calvinists were warned and escaped. Things began to happen. In 1566 Calvinist mobs pillaged churches and monasteries, prompting Philip to send in an army under the Duke of Alva to restore order and 'established' religion. William left silently for Germany to raise an army.

This was the start of the Eighty Years War against Spain, one of the most complex and bloody struggles in European history. Initially, the whole of the Low Countries, Catholic and Protestant, noble and burgher, rose, but the Dutch were helped by longer Spanish lines of communication and the barrier of the great rivers. Alva was brutally successful on land – though his brutality against innocents did a lot to stiffen resistance – but by sea the Dutch 'Sea Beggars'

established a complete mastery. The fighting moved back and forth relentlessly across rivers, fields and dykes, leaving a trail of death and devastation. Towns such as Breda, Haarlem and Zutphen were sacked and recaptured several times. At Leyden and Alkmaar the people breached their own dykes to relieve Spanish sieges. William's skills were vital to the Dutch, and not only as a military strategist: his diplomacy alone managed to hold the ever disputatious provinces together.

In 1576, following the 'Spanish Fury' at Antwerp where unpaid Spanish troops mutinied and slaughtered 7,000 citizens, Alva was replaced and the Pacification of Ghent followed, a triumph for William's moderate policy. However, the Calvinist factions in his own camp could not be controlled indefinitely, and their insistence on the total extermination of Catholicism in the Low Countries led to the Union of Utrecht (1579), which *de facto* established the seven Dutch provinces as a separate nation. In the face of Calvinist intransigence, the Spanish commander, the Duke of Parma, won back the southern, Catholic provinces – i.e., Belgium – for Spain, and the conflict thereafter continued as a Protestant-versus-Catholic war.

William was assassinated in 1584, but his son Prince Maurice, a gifted general, continued the fight. An English expeditionary force under the Earl of Leicester arrived to help, and made a hash of it. When Maurice had done clearing out the Spaniards, the Dutch set up their own East India Company (1602) to use their rapidly developing naval power to snatch at the Spanish and Portuguese monopolies in the spice trade. A West India Company planted settlers at New

Amsterdam (later New York). Spain signed a truce in 1609, but the Thirty Years War saw further conflict, and it wasn't till the Treaty of Westphalia (1648) that Spain recognised the Republic of the Seven United Netherlands as a sovereign state.

The period of the Eighty Years war is one of sustained Dutch endeavour and success. Like the Ancient Greeks, forced by a hostile land on to the sea, their successes in the seventeenth century had their roots well back in their past. Their herring busses had been masters of the North Sea fishing grounds since the Middle Ages, and long remained so. From that, they had gone into the Baltic trade and whaling. Then, as their ships improved, they sailed further and further afield till, forced to it by the Spaniards, they burst upon the world as international shippers with their own growing colonial empire seized from their enemies in the Far East, the Caribbean and South Africa. Their fleets and ships were the envy of foreign monarchs, their seamen were renowned for their skill and bravery, their admirals for their intrepidity and dash – men such as de Ruyter, Piet Heyn, who seized the Spanish treasure fleet off Cuba in 1628, and Tromp, who went to sea at the age of eight and won over thirty victories against the Spanish and the English. Their explorers left Dutch names as far afield as Spitsbergen, Tasmania and Cape Town. Amsterdam replaced Antwerp, in Belgium, as the whole world's entrepôt, the international centre for the reception and distribution of the produce of five continents. Even the Spanish depended on them for grain and naval supplies.

Such wonders for a small damp land of artificial mounds might seem more than enough, but there was more: whatever the field of human skill the Dutch of those years excelled in it. Desiderius Erasmus (1466-1536) was one of the greatest classical scholars of the Renaissance, the father of humanism, of tolerance, in many ways of the Protestant Reformation. There was Hugo Gropius, an international jurist; Christian Huygens, a physicist; Anton van Leeuwenhoek, a pioneer in microscopes; Baruch Spinoza, a great philosopher. There was Rembrandt, Franz Hals, Vermeer, de Hooch, Cuyp: master artists in an age of masters: brilliant practitioners of still life, portraiture, landscapes and realistic portrayals of everyday life. And besides all these famous names there were all the fishermen, the merchants, the colonisers, the universities such as Leiden – attended by scholars from all over Europe, including Protestant refugees such as James Renwick, the Covenanter – and the craftsmen, many of them also refugees – Huguenots from France, Jews from Portugal and Spain – who made Dutch products superior to the rest: pottery, weaving, diamond-cutting, paper-manufacturing, printing, sugar-refining, rope-making. Newspapers were produced in Holland, around 1618: very cosmopolitan Euro-papers they were, with reports in various languages on wars and royal scandals in various parts. Above all, there were the unremembered essential Dutch men and women who made all these notable achievements possible, carrying on the age-old relentless struggle against the sea with their spades and carts and windmills.

It is hardly surprising that the Republic emerged from the Thirty Years War the most prosperous naval country in Europe, as the English found to their cost in the course of three short sharp commercial wars (1652–4, 1665–7, 1672), in the second of which de Ruyter's fleet of eighty ships blockaded the Thames and caused a panic in London. There were political problems between the supporters of the House of Orange-Nassau and the Republicans, resulting in a period without Statdholders, when Johan de Witt was Grand Pensionary. France, under Louis XIV, replaced Spain as the overmighty foreign foe, with Charles II of Britain playing a slippery and impecunious client role to the French King, his paymaster. Eventually, under grave threat of French conquest, the de Witt brothers were murdered by a mob, and William III of Orange, aged twenty-one, was appointed Statdholder and Commander-in-Chief by the States General. William, a brilliant strategist, beat back the French in alliance with the old enemy, Spain, and also managed to find time to marry Mary, Charles II's niece, daughter of the King's brother James, Duke of York. When James succeeded to the throne of Great Britain in 1685, his rashly Catholic policies rapidly alienated his subjects, whereupon they drove him out, and William and Mary were invited to reign in his stead. This rather unlikely Dutchman – who remained throughout primarily concerned with his complex campaigns against Louis XIV – is the famous 'King Billy' celebrated to this day, often with riotous results, in Northern Ireland.

By the eighteenth century, a century and a half of war had clearly exhausted the Dutch, though with Britain she continued an active anti-French role. French fashions and culture spread like the pox as the native culture seemed to droop

with exhaustion. Dutch monopoly of the carrying trade was broken by Bremen, Hamburg and Denmark, and their mercantile interests came to rely rather on British goodwill. Their Indies companies were incompetently run from Amsterdam – and the British had made off with some key colonies, notably New York – but the merchants themselves, whether slave-traders in Africa and the Caribbean or coffee-planters in Java, remained as astute as ever. Thus, with an accumulation of capital but little native investment opportunity, banking and foreign investment flourished during this period, much of the investment being in Britain. It was through Dutch finance houses that the British paid their continental clients and armies in the great wars of the mid-century. This financial interlocking continued till the fourth Anglo-Dutch War (1780–4), caused by British exasperation with Dutch profiteering during the American War of Independence, which proved disastrous for the Dutch, as they had neglected their navy for the previous fifty years. Thereafter the decline became painfully obvious and had immediate political consequences.

The original Republic had rejected democracy in favour of oligarchy. When, in the eighteenth century, this oligarchy of rich merchants ceased to be open to recruits from below and became a self-perpetuating, self-serving, closed shop, the original concept that these oligarchs were in power to serve the interests of the people revived. A Patriot party emerged, supported by rich men who couldn't get their feet under the table. Their chance came with the defeat in 1784: the arch-conservative Statdholder, William V, was blamed. There were riots; William fled, then was reinstated by a Prussian army. The French

Revolution acted as a useful catalyst, with vital support being lent to the Patriots. During the winter of 1794, the freezing of the great rivers allowed the French to get right into the centre of the Netherlands. With their support the Patriots seized power and William fled to England.

Revolutionary France, however, had merely perfected what the *ancien régime* had been trying to do for a century and more. The Dutch Republic was replaced by a French-inspired Batavian Republic, and ancient liberties of place and class were abolished. The Dutch were caught between the French and British millstones. Their economy deteriorated rapidly as the intense British naval blockade, seizure of key colonies – such as the Cape of Good Hope – and French financial exploitation reduced the Netherlands to a merely agricultural country. The decline of the eighteenth century reached a nadir. Prosperous cities became provincial market towns and the old spirit of adventure became a stick-in-the-mud attitude. In 1806, Napoleon made his brother, Louis, King of Holland, and four years later, the Dutch were incorporated into the French Empire.

Fortunately for the Dutch (and a lot of other decent people) the French got the kicking they so richly deserved at Waterloo. The House of Orange-Nassau, in the person of William's son, was restored by the British, and the victorious Powers – who now remade Europe following the Napoleonic period – made him, as William I, King of the whole Low Countries. William, an enlightened despot, put his energies and personal fortune into reviving the economy, but some of his policies exasperated the Belgians, who revolted in 1830 and, unexpectedly gaining British support, became a separate kingdom. William toppled this arrangement by an invasion, but the Powers re-established it, whereupon he abdicated in disgust in 1840.

The nineteenth century saw the inevitable transformation into a democratic parliamentary democracy. The colonies in the East Indies, principally Java, provided a considerable proportion of the national budget until harsh conditions on the coffee plantations led to a liberal humanitarian outcry, after which the conditions improved and the revenue diminished. A colonial war further drained finances. At home, agriculture became specialised in the production of dairy produce and meat, trade and shipping revived, new industries such as coal, textiles and electrical products developed, with Rotterdam becoming the busiest port in Europe, at the centre of much of the new industry. Queen Wilhelmina managed to keep the country out of the First World War, but vigorous attempts to do the same in the sequel led only to Nazi invasion in May 1940. Rotterdam was bombed and reduced largely to rubble. There were some pro-Nazi, anti-Jewish Dutch who collaborated with the Nazis, but most people helped create increasing difficulties for the Germans, who retaliated with their customary executions of hostages, for example in the strike by Amsterdam dockers against Jewish deportations. A Resistance movement created havoc by blowing dykes and flooding vast areas. As the Germans started pulling out, such activities increased, huge battles went on as the Allies moved in, and starvation threatened. In the East, all colonies were overrun by the Japanese.

Since the War, the Dutch, as well as dealing with great floods in 1953, have followed the same paths as most other EC countries. Increased industrialisation – steel, electronics, petro-chemicals – led to affluence in the 1950s and 1960s, and economic recession and unemployment in the 1970s and 1980s. They have been vigorous members of NATO, Benelux, and the EC, which takes some 70 per cent of their exports. Indonesia obtained independence in 1949, all former Dutch colonial subjects having a right to settle in the Netherlands. Despite much government-backed emigration and massive land reclamation in the old Zuider Zee, the rapidly expanding population is a major problem: 413 people per square kilometre, almost twice that of Japan.

Politically, the 'pillarisation' of politics and society is a Dutch phenomenon which might have some significance in tomorrow's Europe. 'Pillarisation' means that the various religious and ideological groups that are never going to agree on fundamentals – such as Catholics, Calvinists and Communists – and who could, if they went to extremes, make the country unworkable, organise their own parties, unions, businessmen's groups and sports clubs. These groupings are then seen as 'pillars', each supporting the nation, separate from the others but recognising the valid role of the other 'pillars' and their right to exist – which is the crucial point. It does tend to keep the Dutch separate from each other, but this is probably a good thing where deep and contentious divisions exist – especially when you're having to share a waterlogged, sinking, man-made world with too many other people.

I DIDN'T LIKE DOING IT, BUT AT LEAST IT STOPPED THEM BLOODY GOOSE-STEPPING.

AND DON'T COME BACK
TILL YOU'VE FOUND IT.

PORTUGAL

Portugal has been a completely independent country since the twelfth century, apart from sixty years of Spanish rule in the sixteenth and seventeenth centuries. The country is a paradox, peripheral, yet central to some of the main themes of European history, innovative, enterprising and wildly successful yet conservative and fatalistic to the point of stultification. Comparisons are odious, but the contrast between Portugal and the Netherlands – who do share some characteristics in history – is stark.

The Portuguese were Iron Age Celts like everyone else at the start, though they had the occasional Mycenaean merchant and Carthaginian recruiting officer passing through on business trips. Here, in 'Lusitania', the Romans met with a stiffer resistance than anywhere else, but by 60 BC Caesar was able to establish the provincial capital at *Olisipio* (now Lisbon). In the south, the Romans established the huge agricultural estates called *latifundia* that have survived in one form or another till the present in Alentejo Province, though in the abortive Communist revolution of 1975 they were collectivised, with catastrophic results. At present, rich Dutch and German farming companies are moving in to 'modernise' agriculture in preparation for 1992: whether they are more successful than the Bolsheviks with the rural population remains to be seen.

Life in Lusitania was uneventful till the collapse of Rome, when it was invaded by Swabians (east Germans), who settled in the north between the Douro and Minho rivers, accounting for the Teutonic types thereabouts. Around AD 585 the Visigoths established an empire throughout the Iberian peninsula, with its capital at Toledo in Spain. Like other barbarian kingdoms of this period it had an elective kingship and tended to fall apart at election times and for prolonged periods thereafter. In 711, one faction conceived the notion of summoning aid from North Africa and within a decade the Moors had conquered almost the whole peninsula.

As far as Portugal was concerned, they settled mainly in the south, especially in the Algarve where the climate is not unlike that of North Africa; the moist green hill country of the north did not attract them. They were considerably more civilized and tolerant than the Visigoths, improved on Roman farming and irrigation techniques, introduced rice, cotton and citrus cultivation and developed urban life.

In the far north of the peninsula, small independent Christian kingdoms

116

" ON THE COLLAPSE OF ROME, PORTUGAL WAS INVADED BY ...EAST GERMANS."

developed in opposition, and one of these, Leon, included the northern, previously Swabian, part of Portugal. This county of Leon was known as 'Portucale', the Roman name for Oporto. King Alfonso VI of Leon took the opportunity provided by the passing visit of some Crusaders to his shrine at Compostela to ask them for help against the Moors, and one of those who took up his offer, Raymond of Burgundy, later married Alfonso's daughter and became heir to the throne of Leon. His cousin, Henry of Burgundy, married another daughter, Teresa, and was given the county of Portucale to govern. In those days, an enterprising knight could rise in the world by deft footwork. When Count Henry died in 1112, his son Afonso Henriques rose in rebellion against Leon in 1128, and thereafter concentrated on expanding his county to the south, taking Lisbon from the Moors in 1147 with Crusader help. Among his helpers – who sacked the city before finally proceeding to the Holy Land – were the first English to come to Portugal, described in a contemporary chronicle as 'plunderers, drunkards and rapists, men not seasoned with the honey of piety', which proves conclusively that today's football hooligans abroad are merely following in a long tradition. One of them, Gilbert of Hastings, stayed behind and got a job as Archbishop of Lisbon. Before he died, Afonso was recognised by the King of Leon as King of Portugal, and by the time of Afonso III in the mid thirteenth century the whole of modern Portugal had been conquered from the Moors.

The reconquest allowed Portugal's kings to lob out vast fiefs to trusted nobles and to the military and holy orders. The first Cortes, the legislative assembly, met in 1211. An outstandingly gifted King, Dinis (1279–1325), in addition to

MUVVER

FRANKLY, DOM ALFONSO,
I FEEL SORRY FOR
THE MOORS.

building some fifty fortresses along the Castillian frontier, saw the potential for a Portuguese merchant navy, and grain, olive oil, wine, salt, salt fish and dried fruit were staple exports in his reign to Flanders, Brittany, Catalonia and England. He founded a university, and reorganised the Templars – then being forcibly abolished elsewhere – as the Order of Christ, responsible to the King instead of to the Pope. Wars against the Spanish kingdom of Castile punctuated the rest of the fourteenth century. On the death of King Fernando in 1383, the last of the original Burgundian dynasty, the King of Castile advanced a strong claim to the crown, but a popular revolt elevated John, Master of Avis, a bastard Burgundian, to the throne. He defeated the Castilians with the help of some English longbowmen at the Battle of Aljubarrota (1385). By the Treaty of Windsor (1386), John married Philippa of Lancaster, daughter of John of Gaunt, Duke of Lancaster and father of the English King Henry IV. The treaty is still in operation more than 600 years later, the longest lasting treaty in European history. Among its beneficial results was Prince Henry the Navigator, the couple's third son.

Having settled the Castilian issue for a season, King John and his successors switched their energies to Morocco, partly for religious, Crusading reasons, partly to keep their barons busy. Morocco was a source of markets and an incentive to adventurous discovery. Casablanca and Tangier were taken. Meanwhile, back at his observatory at Sagres, perched above the craggy cliffs at Cape St Vincent, Prince Henry the Navigator was dispatching expeditions of experimental caravels to explore far down the West African coast to see what, if anything, lay beyond Morocco and in the hope of discovering the sea route to the

Indies and its fabulous spice trade. They reached the tropical forest kingdoms of Guinea and discovered the Cape Verde Islands, Madeira and the Azores. Henry was also Grand Master of the Order of Christ and therefore in a unique position to finance his projects. He brought cartographers, navigators and seamen from many parts of Europe to his School of Navigation, to improve ship building and the sailing of them. If only later Portuguese royalty and ecclesiastics had spent their money as wisely.

After the Prince's death in 1460, the voyages continued. In 1487 Bartholomew Diaz rounded what he called the Cape of Storms and which his King renamed more sanguinely the Cape of Good Hope. Finally, in 1497, came Vasco da Gama's great breakthrough: a voyage into the Indian Ocean, up the East coast of Africa and across to India itself. It was the start of Portugal's Golden Age.

The Portuguese monarchy now rapidly became the richest in Europe, taking a fat 20 per cent of all trading profits. The simultaneously rapid rise in Spanish fortunes sparked by Columbus's voyage led in 1494 to the extraordinary Treaty of Tordesillas, by which the two Iberian powers divided the whole non-European world between them, with papal sanction, along an imaginary line 370 leagues west of the Cape Verde Islands. Not only did this give Portugal the whole of the East, it also gave her a vast windfall that hadn't even been officially discovered at the time: Brazil. By mid sixteenth century, thanks to intrepid explorers and seamen like Afonso d' Albuquerque, Portugal dominated world trade, with strategic trading posts at Goa in India (1510),

Malacca in the East Indies (1511), Ormuz in the Gulf (1515), and Macau in China (1557), to name but a few. Her original foothold on the Guinea coast, besides being a source of gold, allowed her to build up a massive slave trade between West Africa, Europe and Brazil, greatly to the delight of the West African chiefs.

Portugal was the Saudi Arabia of the sixteenth century. The reign of King Manoel I, 1495–1521, marked the country's peak of wealth, elaborate wedding cake buildings decorated with suitable nautical motifs springing up around the country. Basically, Portugal was and remained a small, remote, medieval kingdom, the vast wealth derived from trade profits remaining at the top where it created conspicuous waste and corruption because there were no developed routes – as there were in the Netherlands, for example – for it to filter down to benefit the country as a whole. It hindered the emergence of a proper merchant class and national political institutions because the King could finance whatever he wanted by dipping into profits, without having to beg from or cajole a middle class. Without new men – the kind of men who were modernising the kingdoms of France and England – there could be no new vision, and the lack of new vision is one of the principal disadvantages of isolation. As in most medieval kingdoms in, say, the twelfth century, financial affairs had been left largely to the Jews, who, with the remaining Moors, had been hitherto tolerated. Now their increased wealth attracted popular resentment, and this, together with official pressure from the Spanish Inquisition, led to their expulsion. Significantly, some fled to the Netherlands, a country not entirely lacking in financial and commercial

BUT... DO WE **HAVE** TO HAVE THE BIT WITH **GLASGOW** IN IT?

TREATY OF TORDESILLAS, 1494.

acumen. As a result, Portugal became a country with a vast commercial empire and no commercial expertise.

There was also an increasing lack of manpower. The population was small. It took a great number of men and ships to garrison colonies stretching from Brazil to Macau. Thousands died in shipwrecks, from disease, in battles with natives. By 1570, the whole extraordinary structure was collapsing for want of proper management: the expenses of maintaining it, together with foreign debts, falling commodity prices, foreign competition and a declining domestic agriculture – a consequence of manpower shortage – outweighed the profits. Reckless and broke, the House of Avis went down fighting.

Remote though Portugal was, it had not escaped the chief curse of the sixteenth and seventeenth centuries: religious fanaticism. King Sebastian, desirous of spreading Catholicism regardless of expense, launched a Crusade against the Moroccans only to be wiped out, together with most of his nobles and a large army, at the Battle of Alcazarquivir (1578). His uncle Henry, an aged cardinal, became King, and when he died two years later there were no heirs. Philip II of Spain, with his Habsburg wealth and power, claimed the throne, defeated his rivals, and inaugurated a sixty-year period of unpopular Spanish rule. His successors, Philips III and IV, treated Portugal like a conquered land, ruled it from Madrid and taxed it to pay for Spanish wars. Worst of all, Portugal, as a part of the Spanish Empire, became fair game for attacks from Spain's enemies, England and the Netherlands, who had formerly bought their spices at Lisbon. Her colonies and ships were

seized, and Spain did nothing to defend them. Her trade fell into Dutch and English hands.

Spanish occupation ended in 1640 when Philip IV attempted to raise troops in Portugal to put down rebellion in Catalonia, and a popular uprising made the Duke of Braganza King as John IV. Spain fought, but being preoccupied with the Thirty Years War and nearly bankrupt, eventually acknowledged Portugal's renewed independence (Treaty of Lisbon, 1668). In 1662, King John resumed his country's traditional friendship with England when his daughter, Catherine of Braganza, became Queen to the English monarch Charles II. Charles, an expert on women, was captivated, chiefly by her dowry: £300,000 in cash, Bombay, Tangier, as well as trading privileges in Brazil. 'His Majesty', wrote Clarendon, 'seemed very much affected.' Catherine's retinue of monks and forbidding-looking ladies caused much amusement among the frivolous Restoration courtiers, but she adapted, and the marriage weathered well despite the King's notorious habits. When Charles died in 1685, Catherine returned to Portugal, where she ruled as a wise Regent for another twenty years. The Methuen Treaty (1703) further cemented Anglo-Portuguese relations, ruined the Portuguese textile industry by letting in English cloth at cheap rates and boosted port exports till port became a vital necessity of life for every squire in England.

At the beginning of the eighteenth century, Portugal was still a medieval land, religious intolerance making it unattractive to foreigners. It was even claimed

IT'S A BIG IMPROVEMENT
ON THE ORIGINAL STABLE.

that the climate was unfavourable to begetting children. Even in mid-century, industry, apart from port, hardly existed. The Braganzas, unlike the Bourbons in Spain, did not instil any new energy into their isolated country, and the discovery of gold (1692) and diamonds (1728) in Brazil allowed them to do without both taxes and parliaments. Wealth again flowed into the little country, only to be squandered on lavish and gigantic baroque buildings, such as the enormous convent at Mafra, built by John V between 1717 and 1730, 800 ft across the front and employing 50,000 builders in totally unproductive labour. This was Portugal at its most stagnant, like Ancient Egypt. The same monarch – who ended his long life in 1750 with eight years of total imbecility – spent several fortunes obtaining unbelievably useless privileges from the Pope (who was always glad to relieve him of some of his worldly burdens). He had his private chapel officially pronounced a patriarchate, and obtained the title 'His Most Faithful Majesty'. Portugal had more ecclesiastical establishments than any other country in Europe: it is estimated that about half the population were churchmen of some sort and the Church owned two-thirds of the land and the three universities. The Inquisition was especially active.

As a result, the development of Brazil's mines was undercapitalised, and so was the slave trade, though the Portuguese were by far the most successful of the West Coast slavers, keeping on good terms with the English and buying the best slaves from other nationals' trading posts to keep expenses to a minimum. In East Africa, the Dutch had broken Portugal's trading empire, African risings had expelled them from many of their posts and Arab resurgence had hastened their ruin. Everything north of Zanzibar had vanished, and Mozambique became little more than a few forts on the coast and a host of unreal claims. It was a phantom empire, and Portugal a nation clearly in decay at the accession of Joseph (José) I in 1750.

Sebastian Joseph de Carvalho e Mello, Marquis of Pombal, was the individual who tackled this combination of lost opportunities, idleness and corruption. He had been to England and Vienna as ambassador and had had his eyes opened to eighteenth-century realities. Gaining the complete confidence of King José, Pombal used the absolute royal power to carry out wide reforms of the administration – sacking corrupt and useless sinecurists – and of commerce, reorganising the Brazilian mines, regulating trade on tobacco and sugar and taking over the diamond trade. When a catastrophic earthquake demolished most of Lisbon in 1755, it was Pombal alone who organised the burial of victims and fed the survivors. Later, he rebuilt the city. His ruthlessness, his contempt for the vast useless section of the population comprising the Church and the nobility ensured that he had a multitude of enemies in high places. An assassination attempt on the King in 1758 – some claim Pombal himself engineered it – led to his 'unearthing' evidence sufficient to execute opposition nobles and expel the Jesuits from the country, the effects of which included secularisation of higher education, and sweeping changes in Brazil, where the Jesuits had exercised enormous political power over the native Indians.

Pombal fell from power when the amenable José died, but the subsequent aristocratic reaction in the reign of Maria I (1777–1816) did not destroy his reforms. He had greatly strengthened the state by creating Portugal's version of an enlightened despotism. In 1792, however, Queen Maria went mad for twenty-four years and in 1807, when the country was invaded by Napoleonic armies, the whole royal court left for Brazil, where Maria's son John VI ruled as Prince Regent. As the cause of the French invasion was Portugal's refusal to stop trading with Britain, two British generals, Beresford and Wellington, now stepped into the vacuum to see what they could do to help. The French were forced out by 1811, whereafter Beresford continued as virtual dictator, and the British obtained the right to trade freely with Brazil as their reward, thus ending Portugal's lucrative monopoly. The spread of French Revolutionary ideas led to Brazil becoming an independent kingdom – later an Empire – and a rebellion by Portuguese army officers in 1820, which set a pattern for military coups that ran on till 1926, as the old kingdom and its phantom empire lurched and staggered on into modern times in a welter of incompetence, lethargy and poverty.

The details of this decline are hardly the concern of modern Europe. They included a prolonged civil war between liberals and reactionaries, with the popular and reactionary King Miguel being forced off the throne in 1834 by combined British and French naval intervention. In the second half of the century, the warring factions became institutionalised as political parties, but Republicanism grew as the monarchy proved endlessly feckless and was humiliated by the British and Germans in Africa. In 1910 a military revolt overthrew King Manoel the Unfortunate, who sailed off to exile in Britain, and

was replaced by a Republic that was even worse: sixteen years of political chaos, forty-five military interventions, and complete inability to satisfy even the most modest demands of its supporters.

It is hardly surprising that when General Carmona set up a dictatorship in 1926 it had popular support. In 1928, Dr Salazar, a Professor of Economics, became Finance Minister, taking the job only on condition that he was allowed to control the expenditure of all government departments. Salazar was a strict monetarist, and the economy improved directly. He governed the country till 1968, using the methods of his time just as Pombal had done.

These included only one permitted political party, a secret police trained by Gestapo advisers, detention camps in the Azores and unofficial intervention on Franco's side in the Spanish Civil War. He enjoyed popularity: few people may have benefited financially, but economics isn't everything. Some countries prefer stability and religion safeguarded to loadsamoney: the disapproval of the Western powers didn't mean much to the Portuguese.

The regime only lost credibility at home when the overseas empire started succumbing to the 'winds of change' people said were sweeping through colonial territories after the Second World War. India seized Goa in 1961. A policy of No Concessions in Angola and Mozambique led to civil war there. In 1968 Salazar suffered brain damage when his deck chair collapsed, and he was succeeded by Marcello Caetano. Legend has it that, though the Doctor lingered for another two years, no one dared tell him he wasn't Prime Minister any more. Caetano's attempts to provide limited democracy only allowed air time to underlying dissension, sparked off by the colonial problem and by the spirit of the age. There was growing discontent in the army as young conscripts started to sympathise with the freedom movements they were sent to Africa to suppress.

In 1974, with the African situation deteriorating rapidly, Major de Carvalho led a bloodless coup which precipitated two years of revolutionary turmoil, which generals were powerless to control. The granting of immediate independence to the colonies meant the arrival of one and a half million bitter, destitute colonial refugees. There were many coup attempts, nationalisation of banks, Communism, collectivisation of the great estates and confiscation of foreign property. There was complete chaos. The Archbishop of Braga summoned Catholics of the north to the struggle of Christ against Satan.

Then came an election, a victory for Mario Soares and his Socialist party, followed by an army putsch. The result is currently a popular President Soares and efforts to clean up the economic mess. There is widespread unemployment, stagnation, trade deficits, and many companies often fail to pay their workers. Foreign capital is slowly being encouraged back after its initial flight. Modernisation of agriculture is imperative, say the experts, if Portugal is to be anything more than a 'peripheral curiosity' after 1992. But the farmers of Alentejo province are hard to convince.

SPAIN

Before time began there were civilizations in Spain: Paleolithic cave painters and advanced Neolithic societies. Before 1100 BC there was the trading city of Tartessus, mentioned in the Old Testament as Tarshish, situated somewhere near the mouth of the Guadalquivir. From here, Iberian seamen sailed northwards to the Scily Isles after tin to alloy with their native copper into bronze. Still before 1100 BC, the Phoenicians came, attracted by the thriving metal industry, the rich fishing and the purple dye trade. They built colonies: Cadiz was one of them, a European city over three thousand years old.

It took the Romans over 200 years to conquer Hispania after Scipio Africanus ended Carthaginian power in 206 BC. Caesar smashed his rival Pompey here, at the Battle of Lerida in 49 BC. The Roman contribution to Spain was immense, including the language, cities, aqueducts, roads, bridges, laws, baths and basilicas. In return Spain gave not only soldiers and produce, but emperors

(Trajan, Hadrian, Theodosius) and writers such as Seneca, Lucan, Martial and Quintilian.

Spain was comparatively lucky in its Dark Ages conquerors. The Visigoths, who wiped out the others, were considered allies of Rome and remained a fairly small minority of the population, constituting a military caste with its own law and social structure. When their king and his nobles switched from the doctrines of Arius of Alexandria to the Catholic church the way was open for a merger between them and the native Romano-Spanish population. The capital was fixed at Toledo. The Visigoth's chief legacy was their establishment of a single Spanish kingdom – that and the concept of blue blood, said to have been derived from the prominent veins on Visigothic chiefs.

In common with other Dark Age types, however, the Visigoths had an elective monarchy, which usually meant that elections were major political upheavals. The disputed election of King Roderick in AD 711 proved more fatal than most, when one of the factions invited the support of the Moors from across the water in North Africa. There had been Moorish incursions into Spain even in Roman times, but now, with the fire of Islam in their hearts they went through the leaderless kingdom like the proverbial hot scimitar, under their leader Tariq ibn Ziyad, Governor of Tangier. Within a very few years, almost the whole of Spain had fallen, and the Pillars of Hercules had become Mount Tariq, or Gibraltar (Jebel el Tariq).

The Moorish conquest lasted from 711 till 1492, although from the mid-thirteenth century onwards it had been reduced mainly to Granada in the south. It shattered the Visigothic unity of Spain, replacing it with a multiplicity of Moorish states and tiny Christian kingdoms. It introduced a new religion, a new legal framework, a new language and new races: Arabs and Jews. At its height during the Caliphate of Abd er Rahman (765–88) it possessed a cultural vitality unique to Dark Age Europe, enriched by visiting Islamic scholars, poets, historians and by Andalusians going on pilgrimage to Mecca and returning with new ideas. The government, whilst it didn't lack for the occasional tyrant and zealot, was tolerant of other cultures and religions: efficient taxation was the worst consequence of the conquest for most of its subjects. Not even Charlemagne – defeated at the epic Battle of Roncesvalles in the Pyrenees (778) – could dent Moorish supremacy in the time of Abd er Rahman.

The tiny Christian kingdoms in remote, unconquered parts of the northern mountains now had approximately 800 years of reconquest on their hands. Theirs is a fascinating history, but the fragmentary pattern is impossible to detail here. They had all the problems of medieval Europe – overmighty barons, wars for hegemony, dynastic feuds, poverty and the Church – as well as the Moorish occupation and the political and cultural isolation that went with it. In periods of Moorish decline, they made big advances: in periods of Moorish revival they were pushed back. At the end of 800 years, they had the finest infantry in Europe, but Spain had become a land of fractured, fierce and mutually antipathetic loyalties to match its fractured geography, a nation whose only unity was hatred of infidels.

As a sample of the complexities of Spain's Middle Ages, Sancho the Great, King of Navarre (1000–36), was the first of the petty kings to lord it over the rest. His advantages included the shrine of St James of Compostella – the biggest tourist attraction of its time – and being on the border, open to French influences and occasional support. Following his defeat of Bermudo III, King of Leon, Sancho modestly proclaimed himself Emperor, but died the following year, whereupon his empire split in the accustomed manner amongst his sons. One of his grandsons, Alfonso VI, King of Leon (1065–1109), became also King of Castile when his brother, the King of Castile, happened to be murdered. He then set out to conquer the Muslims – who were themselves equally fragmented – his main advantage for this task being one Rodrigo Diaz de Vilar, El Cid, the greatest of Spain's countless heroes. By 1085 they had conquered as far south as Toledo, where Alfonso had himself crowned Emperor of the Two Regions. The fall of Toledo, however, caused the remaining Muslim states to invite the Almoravids – a fanatical North African group – to come and help them, which they did, defeating Alfonso at the Battle of Zalacca (1086) and also gobbling up the petty Muslim states. El Cid successfully defended Valencia against them till his death in battle, whereafter the Almoravids regained the whole of eastern Spain as far north as Zaragoza, i.e. on the borders of Navarre.

Gradually, two kingdoms, Aragon and Castile – land of castles – emerged pre-eminent, but both of them were basically confederations of smaller kingdoms and so remained, with bewildering local variations. In Aragon,

I CAN LIVE WITH THE NOISE AND THE LITTER, BUT DO THEY HAVE TO CHUCK THEIR HOLY WATER BOTTLES AT THE SHEEP?

roughly eastern Spain, the king was first among equals, if he was lucky, and the barons had in several parts complete feudal power, even to declare their own wars. In Castile, roughly western Spain, the monarchy was constitutionally absolute and the magnates were merely *ricoshombres* (rich guys), though in northern Castile there was also a vast class of minor nobles called *hidalgos* who were – like minor nobles in Scotland – often poor and needy. In both kingdoms wool exported to the markets in Flanders was the main source of wealth, financial transactions being largely in Jewish hands in the reconquered areas, in Italian hands elsewhere. Both Aragon and Castile had been involved at times in wider European affairs at various times, but only on the fringes: Aragon's links with the papacy had secured it a toehold in southern Italy after the demise of the Hohenstaufen: Alfonso the Wise of Castile had foolishly got himself elected Holy Roman Emperor in 1257, thereby sparking off a 200-year financial struggle in Castile with his *ricoshombres* which dragged in a variety of guest stars over the years, including the Black Prince and Bertrand du Guesclin. This struggle was still in progress when Queen Isabella's marriage to Ferdinand of Aragon in 1469 brought modern Spain into being.

The result was a Union of the Crowns, as later in Britain, but in Spain it comprised approximately twenty two Crowns as well as, after 1492, when the last Moorish king was driven from Spain, a large population of Moors, Jews and Moriscos (Moorish converts to Christianity).

Ferdinand and Isabella were astutely aware that they had to establish the power of the Crown completely if the Union was going to last. Their methods included royal control of ecclesiastical patronage, exclusion of great nobles from the administration – hidalgo lawyers substituted – the setting up of numerous legislative royal councils and the backing of any new venture that looked like coining an honest doubloon or two for the royal pair. In this last they were spectacularly lucky, when the loan of three little leaky ships and some jailbirds to Christopher Columbus – generally reckoned a Genoese, but some aver he was an Andalusian Jew – resulted in his reaching of the New World.

Among their councils was the Council of the Inquisition, basically an astute attempt by the Crown to profit from popular envy of the Jews. It was a success, however, that rapidly became a cancer. Moorish Spain had been one of the few places in Europe where Jews could live in peace and prosper. In return, they had served Spain and its multitude of kings, caliphs, emirs and princes well. Much of Spanish literary, artistic, architectural and religious vitality was due, and continued to be due, to them. Their richer members had for long intermarried with the nobility and their blood flowed in the Royal Family itself. Inevitably, as elsewhere, their prosperity attracted ignorant envy, and their religion generated ignorant fears and hatred in a land that had been fighting infidels as a way of life for 800 years. Ferdinand and Isabella saw their opportunity; decisive action against Jews would both be profitable and gain them popularity. They obtained a Bull from Pope Sixtus IV setting up the Inquisition as a Royal Court to deal with the supposed evil influence of Jews: only later did the Pope realise what he had done. As it developed, it acquired the same terror and corrupt absolute power that twentieth-century totalitarian institutions acquired. It also generated horror and revulsion in other European countries, giving Spain a bad name that it has never fully recovered from. Huge numbers of trained informers were exempt from normal law courts. It had secret procedures, used torture, and accused persons had no right to confront hostile witnesses. It rapidly became one of the strongest weapons in the armoury of royal absolutism, generating terror in the population at large.

The results included the immediate expulsion of 170,000 Jews at the very moment in her history when Spain needed all the financial expertise it could get. The religious and racial attitudes the Inquisition fostered led directly to the mad Spanish obsession with 'purity of blood'. Philip II approved statutes excluding 'tainted' persons from ecclesiastical office because 'all the heresies in Germany, France and Spain have been sown by descendants of Jews'. (He was one himself.) Naturally, the Protestant Reformation didn't get a look in. Society became progressively blighted by a fictitious belief that personal honour depended on racial purity and religious orthodoxy: such beliefs stifled initiative, creating both material and spiritual poverty.

About 300,000 Jewish converts to Catholicism remained, always in danger, constituting a major proportion of the intelligentsia, including St Teresa, St John of God, humanists (till suppressed), jurists, defenders of South American Indians, writers, priests and friars of more than common grace.

As for the newly conquered Moors of Granada, Isabella offered them generous terms and religious freedom, which they accepted, then her clerics

had them forcibly converted or expelled. The converts, Moriscos, thereafter remained an alien and depressed community, none of the limitless fortunes from the New World being spent on their promised education and development.

In the New World, Spain carved out a vast colonial Empire stretching from California to Tierra del Fuego, from Cuba to the Philippines. The fabled *conquistadores* – their history and amazing adventures a subject in itself – were, like Drake and Raleigh, ruthless pursuers of gold, power and status, yet there were also many Spanish Dominicans, Franciscans and Jesuits who were actively concerned with the moral problems of conquest, conversion and the government of heathen peoples. By royal decree, all trade was to be carried on through Seville and reserved for Castilians – because Castilian money and blood had carved out the Empire – but the Castilians were incapable of profiting from this monopoly. In effect, Italian and German financiers and suppliers provided what the Castilians couldn't, and other European powers regarded the trade as fair game. Following the development of new extraction processes in the 1540s, silver mining became the major industry in Mexico and Peru, the huge imports of specie exacerbating an existing inflation. Of all the treasure shipped from the slave mines of the New World hardly any of it was invested in the Spanish economy. As in Portugal, a vast amount went on display, grandiose palaces and cathedrals or to pay for imports of items that could better have been produced in Spain, or to satisfy the government's creditors in Italy, Germany or the

Netherlands. Above all, it was spent on Habsburg wars. Spain itself remained a poor, undeveloped country.

The succession of Ferdinand's grandson Charles in 1516 – son of his daughter Juanna the Mad and Philip of Habsburg – diverted Spain from development as a nation state into the role of European and world mega-power. The grandeur, the military commands, the vice-royalties, the wars, the religious orthodoxy all appealed to Spanish grandees: it was all a lot better than developing one's huge estates and – once the popular revolts were put down that greeted Charles's original taxes to pay for his foreign wars – the taxpayers paid for everything. Nobles paid no taxes.

The history of Spain from now on is not the history of good housekeeping. Philip II (1556–98) inherited a debt of 20 million ducats along with his father's worldwide territories and unfinished wars. Despite immense annual shipments of New World silver, he went bankrupt thrice, his armies and navies swallowing the lot and more. Philip convinced himself – if no one else – that the cause of Spain was also the Cause of God, and sensible compromise, such as that of Henry of Navarre in France, was with Philip totally out of the question. Hence the war in the Netherlands went on for eighty years: Spanish armies were not just there to put down rebels, they were there to root out heresies. At the same time, Philip was also fighting Anti-Christ in the shape of the Turks in the Mediterranean – where a significant naval victory by the combined fleets of Spain, Venice and the papacy at the Battle of Lepanto (1571) gave Castilian pride a shot in the arm and presumably made them keener to fork out. In Portugal, following the failure of massive bribes and intrigues on the death of old King

BEG YOUR PARDON, DON HERNAN, BUT YOU CAN'T SHOOT QUETZAL BEFORE 12 TH AUGUST.

Henry, the Duke of Alva was sent in with an army to take the kingdom (1580). Then there were the English and the French: they were the reasons the Dutch were able to hold out against the invincible might of Spain. Against Protestant England therefore, in 1588, Philip launched the Armada of 130 ships and 30,000 men, giving its commander, the Duke of Medina Sidonia, the impossible task of conveying Parma's army in the Netherlands across to England. The resultant shambles cost Philip 10 million ducats. Against France, endless wars and intrigues throughout his reign ended with the Treaty of Vervins in 1598, which merely re-established the position as it had been in 1559. Philip also financed the Counter-Reformation, the Jesuit Order founded by Ignatius Loyola in 1539, and the spread of Catholicism throughout the Spanish Empire.

From the sixteenth to the seventeenth century, called the Golden Century by Spanish historians, the period was far from golden for 95 per cent of the population. Desperate risings were put down with ferocity. It was, however, a time of great literature, great artists – El Greco, Murillo, Velázquez – and the evolution of baroque architecture, an exception to the rule that says culture cannot flourish under repressive regimes.

The writers, including Fernando de Roja, a Jewish convert who brought out the world's first novel, *Celestina* in 1499, Cervantes, and the playwright Lope de Vega, certainly responded more realistically to the spirit of contemporary Spain than its ruling classes and clerics: their works depict a rich variety of crooks, conmen and crackpots who will do anything rather than work.

From Philip's time it was downhill all the way. Philip III (1599–1621)

YOUSE IS LUCKY GENTS. JUST 25 LEAGUES TO THE CITY OF EUROPEAN CULTURE!

undermined efficient government by allowing grandees to hold positions in it. There was rampant inflation, debasement of the currency, 500,000 died of plague, 275,000 Moriscos were expelled, causing an acute labour shortage. Spanish armies controlled Italy, Flanders and the Rhineland, whilst Spanish bribes, subsidies and Jesuit confessors made clients of politicians throughout Europe in the Cause of God. Bankruptcy forced a truce with the Dutch.

The Thirty Years War, during the reign of Philip IV (1621–65) saw war costs soaring – they even had to pay the Dutch, their enemies, to supply food to Spanish armies – more bad money, more bankruptcy, more tax, and various efforts by the King's minister, the Count-Duke of Olivares, to reform the economy – which came to nothing because the Castilians were unwilling to change. Portugal threw off Spanish rule, the Catalans revolted and had their ancient liberties restored and there were popular revolts in Naples and Palermo. The French finished the Spanish army's legendary reputation for invincibility at the Battle of Rocroi (1643) and, by the final Treaty of the Pyrenees (1659), Spain lost Artois, in Belgium, and other areas to France. It was clear to the rest of Europe that the Spanish Empire was tottering.

Charles II (1665–1700), the last of the Spanish Habsburgs, was incapable of ruling, an unfortunate physical degenerate without progeny, whose reign has been accurately described as 'an uninterrupted series of calamities'. The population of Castile declined from $8\frac{1}{2}$ million to $6\frac{1}{2}$ million, estates went untended as nobles virtually wrote their own government subsidies and industry lacked both labour and investment. No one had any money. Louis XIV sliced off more bits of Belgium, then, observing he stood a good chance of grabbing the whole Empire as Charles declined, he desisted and prepared for what was to come. Government was carried out by priestcraft, cabals, intrigues, exorcism and blood feuds. There were riots in the streets of Madrid. Spain's terrible weakness was clear to all Europe.

The War of the Spanish Succession (1700–13) was one of those complicated European wars that fill the textbooks. Charles II left Spain in his will to Philip, Duke of Anjou (reigned 1700–46), Louis XIV's grandson. The Austrian Habsburgs contested this with their Habsburg claimant, the Archduke Charles, and in this they were supported by England, the Netherlands and Savoy, none of whom wanted the vast power of Bourbon France extended all over the Spanish Empire. Whilst the French suffered some setbacks at the hands of the Duke of Marlborough and Prince Eugene of Savoy, they managed to hold on to Spain, despite invasions, Madrid twice occupied and pro-Habsburg revolts in Aragon and Catalonia – where the Archduke had his capital at Barcelona. French bureaucrats were brought in to begin a reform of the chaotic and medieval administration, but it was a disastrous war for Spain. She lost all her European possessions: Belgium, Luxemburg, Milan, Sardinia and Naples. Most humiliating of all, the British obtained Gibraltar.

The Bourbon kings and the talented ministers they employed – such as Ensenada and Carvajal – tried hard to make government more efficient and the economy more productive, but tradition and stagnation remained the

YOU'RE LUCKY HE WASN'T
FIGHTING THE BLOODY
MOROCCANS.

stumbling blocks. The previous system of rule through a large number of legislative councils remained, with their multiple and dilatory bureaucracies. There were different sets of laws for different classes. Valiant attempts to reform the tax system met with the immovable opposition of the privileged and the placemen. The navy was reformed, but it lacked manpower. Basically, any change was regarded by the Spaniards as foreign degeneracy, and at the heart of this attitude was the Church – or as the Duke of Wellington was later to remark: 'The real power in Spain is the clergy.'

Attempts to expand the commercial possibilities of the overseas Empire led to conflict with Britain – such as the War of Jenkins' Ear (1739) over illegal British trading in South America – but the basic problem remained that Spain could not supply what her colonists wanted, so contrabandistas were more than welcome there. The British occupation of Havana during the Seven Years War in 1762 made the point gallingly clear: eleven ships had used the harbour in the previous year, but during an eleven-month period of British occupation 700 ships used it. Colonials visiting Europe found Madrid a meaner city than many of their own. Resentment mounted that their development was monopolised by a country that was herself underdeveloped.

The French Revolution and Napoleon were not problems Spain was able to cope with. The government of Charles IV was in the hands of his wife's paramour Godoy, a youthful officer. His declaration of war on France when Louis XVI was guillotined brought the revolutionaries in from the north and the spread of revolutionary ideas in Catalonia. He then allied with the French against the British, which immediately cut Spain off from her colonies. Next, with the French, he invaded Portugal (1801) but the French took the opportunity to occupy some fortresses on the way there and generally behaved with insufferable Frenchness. When Spain's fleet was smashed at Trafalgar (1805), an alliance of nobles replaced Godoy and King Charles with Ferdinand VII, Charles's son. Napoleon summoned both kings to Bayonne, forced both to abdicate, and appointed his brother Joseph to the job.

Joseph had some support from those who hoped he'd make a better job of it than his predecessors, but there were spontaneous risings against the French which Napoleon seriously underestimated. Areas not strictly controlled by French troops were organised by patriotic juntas and the British advanced from Portugal under Wellington. These two unlikely allies worked well together and smashed the Napoleonic forces at the Battles of Talavera (1809) and Vittoria (1813), the war – called in Spain the War of Independence – proving a major factor in the downfall of the monstrous Frenchman, and called by him his 'Spanish ulcer'. A liberal constitution was produced, which proposed a constitutional monarchy, a Cortes without privileges for nobles and clergy, a modern centralised administration and the abolition of the Inquisition, among other things. Unfortunately, a pattern for Spanish politics now also emerged that came to be followed with monotonous regularity for most of the nineteenth century and beyond: anti-clerical reformers, denounced by their opponents as foreign-inspired atheists and devils, alternated with conservatives to the

LET US FORGET GIBRALTAR, SEÑOR, AND REMEMBER JEREZ.

VIVA ESPAÑA

accompaniment of much violence and frequent military interventions called *pronunciamentos*.

Ferdinand VII, restored on Napoleon's downfall, attempted and failed to reconquer the South American colonies, which had declared their independence during the war. In 1820 a *pronunciamento*, backed by masonic liberals, restored the Constitution, but extremist liberal attacks on monasteries resulted in French intervention, the fall of the liberal government and the revolt of Mexico. Conservative ministers proving incapable, Liberal ones had to be brought in by the King, whereupon arch-Conservatives broke with him and became Carlists – supporters of Ferdinand's reactionary brother Don Carlos. When Ferdinand died and his daughter Isabella II was declared Queen, the First Carlist War (1833–9) broke out, a savage civil war which the Liberal government of Queen Isabella financed by selling Church lands, which, by privatisation, caused a lot of rural unemployment, peasants ejected from these estates by new owners drifting to the towns and providing support for reactionary movements such as the Carlists and later the Anarchists. The War discredited politicians generally; *pronunciamentos* followed thick and fast.

Despite this hopeless government, foreign investment had sparked off economic expansion. Railways created a national market for the first time, to the benefit of industry and agriculture. In the towns a bourgeoisie emerged, though in the countryside the vast feudal estates of negligent grandees persisted with local variations. In Galicia in the north, peasants lived on potatoes grown on Irish-style minute patches and also went in for Irish-style boycotts and rick burnings. Emigration to South America was rife. The Rio Tinto copper mines provided some with employment, financed and run by Scots and Welsh who often wore pith helmets and shorts as if they were out in the Raj. Basque and Catalan industrialists set up the first national banks: they also developed national alliances of industrialists to combat the growth of trade unionism.

A period of stable, broad-based government, called O'Donnell's Liberal Union – after one Leopoldo O'Donnell, leader of a *pronunciamento* in 1854 – presided over this little economic miracle, but Isabella refused to work sensibly with it. Eventually, General Prim y Prats led a revolt based on widespread discontent with the monarchy, and the idiotic, overweight Queen trundled off to France.

General Prats conceded universal suffrage and religious freedom in the constitution of 1869, and searched the pages of the *Almanac de Gotha* for a suitable constitutional monarch – his attempts to persuade a Hohenzollern to ascend the throne helped cause the Franco-Prussian War of 1870 – and eventually came up with Amadeus, Duke of Aosta, who was as good as anyone else. Unfortunately, the intrepid Prats was now assassinated. Amadeus attempted gamely to rule as a constitutional monarch in a land where no one had any idea what a constitutional monarch was, then abdicated in 1873. The Cortes declared a Republic, whereupon a number of confused revolts broke out, during which the excesses of the Republicans and Anarchists increased support for the Conservatives and Carlists. General Serrano seized power and the Bourbon

monarchy was brought back in the person of Alfonso XII, son of Isabella.

A new constitution took account of the obvious fact that as yet Spain was not quite ready for democratic parliamentarianism. The work of the noble Canovas de Castillo, it set up a fake parliamentary game of ins and outs, in which elections were fixed beforehand by wheeler-dealing among local party bosses called *Caciques* – hence the name of this system, *Caciquismo* – who endeavoured to keep the voters sweet by promises and occasional goodies, making use of their ignorance, apathy and gullibility to keep things running smoothly. (Sounds like our own dear system). Radical parties, such as the emerging Socialists and the Anarchists, were rigorously excluded from the system, the goodies, and from office. It worked, in its own way, but like everything else in Spain it was an artificial construct imposed from above and lacking in any form of popular participation.

It partly explains the growth of popular support for Anarchism at this period and its later offshoot Anarcho-Syndicalism, an anti-Marxist proletarian movement that split the labour movement in Spain, and appealed also because it was individualistic, Luddite, and adopted policies that the proletariat wanted. For the Anarchist, modern bourgeois politics was something to be violently overthrown, and the Revolution would be a spontaneous act of the masses. The ballot box was a bourgeois device to enslave workers; the bomb was the answer to it. Obviously, Anarchism was very much a product of Spanish history and Spanish predilections. They were proletarian Carlists. Their party conferences were total anarchy.

The economy continued to expand under *Caciquismo*, but the system took increasing stick for the continuing decline of Spanish power. In 1898 a complete defeat by the United States – called 'The Disaster' in Spain – lost them the remainder of the Empire – Cuba, Puerto Rico and the Philippines – whilst most other European states, including newcomers such as Italy and Belgium that had once been part of the Spanish Empire were now carving out colonial territories. The Catalans were kicking up as usual, their growing demands for autonomy being voiced by leading Catalan intellectual Prat de la Riba. The First World War caused a boom as the belligerents bargained for Spanish raw materials but 1918 brought a resultant collapse. It also brought fresh hope for the proletariat with the Bolshevik Revolution in the USSR.

The post-war period was characterised by a general feeling, from Alfonso XIII downwards, that Spain was long past its best; everyone was fed up with politicians, but the way they had the system sewn up meant they were apparently as irreplaceable as they were useless. In July 1921, a conscript army was massacred in Morocco by Abd el Krim and his tribesmen.

Spanish Morocco, acquired as a protectorate in 1912, was a totally undeveloped, disastrous place for Europeans, who tended to be either murdered or

castrated there. Progressive elements in the army had long wished to conquer and pacify it properly, but the politicians had remained indifferent. The result of the massacre – the Battle of Annual – was an embittered officer corps of *Africanistas*. They created a Legion, or Tercio, on the lines of the French Foreign Legion, with iron discipline, higher pay and a special mystique, which rapidly became the army's crack force. One of the founders of the Tercio was Francisco Franco.

The last Liberal government of the *Caciquismo* period relinquished power in 1923 when General Primo de Rivera (1923–1930) seized power 'in the interests of national salvation'. He was widely popular, meant well, and tried hard. Public works programmes created roads, more railways, hydro-electric schemes, irrigation and tourism. Abd el Krim was defeated. But his proposals for tax reform alienated the rich: as far as they were concerned Primo was in power to protect them, not cut away their age-old privileges. At the same time, he came under attack from the left, whose intellectuals were undergoing something of a cultural renaissance and whose venomous propaganda helped to undermine the regime. The deployment of squads of bicycling police to remove their seditious grafitti was a futile response – the writing was truly on the wall for Primo. With dwindling support from the King and the army, and the adverse effects of the International Slump, Primo de Rivera resigned. The following year, April 1931, amid confusion and cries for a republic, Alfonso XIII packed his bags and left.

The Second Republic was a shambles: there were eighteen governments in five years. What was new was mass politics. Tensions between rich and poor, Catholic and anti-Catholic that had festered for centuries in small towns no one had ever bothered about were suddenly politicised with dramatic and violent results as party organisers arrived by train, mule and motor car to hold mass demonstrations and whip up the expectations of the gullible with promises of a utopia to arrive shortly. The conservative classes regarded this with horror, taking the sudden explosion of hot air as a prelude to Bolshevik revolution. Every one wanted the country modernised: but the Slump caused a 75 per cent fall in exports, industrial stagnation and rising unemployment. About thirty political parties, each one split internally, formed and reformed themselves in ephemeral coalitions, while violence and church-burning increased and contentious legislation legalising divorce, pornography, secular education incensed Catholic and conservative Spain. Catalonia revolted, once again. The proletariat in Asturias set up a Socialist Republic defended by a 'Red Army'. Carlist Navarre was in training to defend Catholicism. The Falange militia was founded. Rhetoric and calls for bloody revolution inflamed every situation.

The conservative, anti-Bolshevik rising began in July 1936, led by junior officers who aimed to rescue the nation from 'government in the gutter'. Franco's African troops gave the rising teeth. The resulting Civil War (1936–39) was and remains one of the stark quintessentials of twentieth-century Europe, both sides – Nationalists (Conservatives) and Republicans (Leftists) – displaying great heroism, great violence, great men and women, great principles and having powerful backers who were merely using the occasion and the suffering of the Spanish nation to test their own brands of evil.

In Republican areas, workers' militias led by elected officers whose every

order had to be discussed and voted on before it could be obeyed, replaced local government. 'Power lay in the streets,' said Dolores Ibarruri, 'the whole state aparatus was destroyed.' Thousands of priests were shot and churches burnt. In the Nationalist zones, workers' leaders were likewise slaughtered. The Republicans were split from the beginning amongst various groupings of Anarchists, Socialists and Trotskyites from which the Communists rapidly emerged as leaders, due partly to their expertise at propaganda, partly because they controlled the all-important Soviet arms supplies. As the only recognisably stable force on the left they attracted support from non-Communists. Catalonia and other places issued their own money. In Aragon they set up a utopia of agrarian collectives (later destroyed by the Communists). Santander had its own diplomats in London. This 'revolutionary cantonalism' – in other words traditional Spanish fragmentalism – made it impossible for the Republicans to run their war effort or their economy effectively. The Communists took control by the normal Communist methods: murder, secret police terror, lying propaganda and the ruthless promotion of party members.

On the Nationalist side, Franco rapidly secured control over all the forces of the right. His first cabinet in 1938, contained three generals, one Carlist, two Falangists, two technocrats and two ministers from the old Conservative party. A fair reflection of his support, or as dear Adolf put it: 'The clerical monarchist scum are floating to the top'. With a rigid command structure, the war economy of the Nationalist areas was well organised: wages were fixed, inflation controlled, foreign exchange rates guaranteed, the church was in full control of education, there were moral decrees against, for example, 'immodest dress', libraries were purged, leftists were sacked: and a genuine reflection of what Franco stood for, ridding Spain of modern decadence and Bolshevism. The sincerity with which he held his beliefs drove his ally Hitler up the wall.

In April 1937 Guernica, a small Basque town, was destroyed by the bombs of the German Condor Legion killing 1600 and wounding thousands more. The raid was counter-productive: the Republican side was given a tremendous moral boost and they won the sympathies of the world's press. The image of Guernica has endured in Picasso's picture and countless works of literature – as a symbol of the horrors of Fascism. Blitzes came into fashion for the first time. African troops were air-lifted. Hitler, Mussolini and Stalin were having a dress rehearsal.

Inevitably, Franco, having failed initially to take Madrid, cut the Republican area in two, concentrating to begin with on the north, where the resources lay. Despite their undoubted bravery, the Republicans' disorganisation, internecine feuds and accumulating defeats did for them in the end. They spent their final months denouncing each other and having coups while their supporters deserted them.

Franco ruled Spain from 1939 till 1975. Despite its corporate state image, its fascist trappings and its chumminess with the Axis in World War Two, the regime was not fascist. Neither was his sending Spanish units to help Hitler attack the Soviet Union: Spain had been fighting Anti-Christ from time immemorial. It was conservative, Catholic, authoritarian: arguably, it was sound government of a type that made sense in Spain, and Spain has not had a lot of sound government. It rested, say the experts, on the apathy of the masses, but what government – apart from a police state – doesn't?

The Civil war had ruined the economy, as well as being a major, disfiguring wound that is still hard to forget. After 1945, Spain was boycotted as Hitler's ally by the West, till in the 1950s the United States came to terms with Franco as a sound anti-Communist. Thereafter, economic development planned mainly by technocrats of the Catholic *Opus Dei* movement was funded by foreign loans, tourism and the remittances of Spaniards working abroad in France and West Germany. It was like water in a dry parched land. Agricultural and social changes were slow, but they did come, and increased prosperity allowed ordinary citizens to enjoy luxuries long denied them. Gradually, though the Caudillo kept his firm hand on everything throughout the period, a division emerged between Francoists who saw change as betrayal of all they had fought for and reformists who sought some liberalisation. With Franco's death in 1975 change was inevitable, and problems of transition between then and the elections of 1977 were handled by the General's chosen heir, King Juan Carlos, with considerable skill.

Consensus politics continues, with governments still sprinkled with reformed Francoists. The main problems are: (1) regional breakaway movements, such as Basque separatism; (2) high expectations not fulfilled; (3) rapid social change as a result of economic boom, and the overturning of traditional moral values resulting from the opening up to Western Europe and the liberalisation of the Catholic Church after the Second Vatican Council; and economic problems common to Europe in the last decade or so.

Spain without serious and age-old problems would not be Spain, but the possibility is here today, a possibility built on Spanish blood and the terrible divisions of history, for Spain to become something more constructive, more relevant and worthy of the enduring tenacity and Christian values of her people.